D1325155

Foreign Lang. — A
a guide to goo

The *Pathfinder* Series

Active learning — listening and reading

Reading for pleasure in a foreign language (PF2)
Ann Swarbrick   ISBN 0 948003 98 7

Developing skills for independent reading (PF22)
Iain Mitchell & Ann Swarbrick   ISBN 1 874016 34 8

Creative use of texts (PF21)
Bernard Kavanagh & Lynne Upton   ISBN 1 874016 28 3

Listening in a foreign language (PF26)
A skill we take for granted?
Karen Turner   ISBN 1 874016 44 5

Supporting learners and learning

Teaching learners how to learn
Strategy training in the ML classroom (PF31)
Vee Harris   ISBN 1 874016 83 6

Making effective use of the dictionary (PF28)
Gwen Berwick and Phil Horsfall   ISBN 1 874016 60 7

Nightshift (PF20)
Ideas and strategies for homework
David Buckland & Mike Short   ISBN 1 874016 19 4

Grammar matters (PF17)
Susan Halliwell   ISBN 1 874016 12 7

Planning and organising teaching

Assessment and planning in the MFL department
(PF29)
Harmer Parr   ISBN 1 874016 71 2

Departmental planning and schemes of work (PF11)
Clive Hurren   ISBN 1 874016 10 0

Fair enough? (PF14)
Equal opportunities and modern languages
Vee Harris   ISBN 1 874016 03 8

Making the case for languages (PF8)
Alan Moys & Richard Townsend   ISBN 0 948003 79 0

Bridging the gap (PF7)
GCSE to 'A' level
John Thorogood & Lid King   ISBN 0 948003 89 8

Improve your image (PF15)
The effective use of the OHP
Daniel Tierney & Fay Humphreys   ISBN 1 874016 04 6

Teaching/learning in the target language

On target (PF5)
Teaching in the target language
Susan Halliwell & Barry Jones   ISBN 0 948003 54 5

Keeping on target (PF23)
Bernardette Holmes   ISBN 1 874016 35 5

Motivating all learners

Yes — but will they behave? (PF4)
Managing the interactive classroom
Susan Halliwell   ISBN 0 948003 44 8

Not bothered? (PF16)
Motivating reluctant language learners in Key Stage 4
Jenifer Alison   ISBN 1 874016 06 2

Communication re-activated (PF6)
Teaching pupils with learning difficulties
Bernardette Holmes   ISBN 0 948003 59 6

Differentiation (PF18)
Taking the initiative
Anne Convery & Do Coyle   ISBN 1 874016 18 6

Cultural awareness

Crossing frontiers (PF30)
The school study visit abroad
David Snow & Michael Byram   ISBN 1 874016 84 4

Languages home and away (PF9)
Alison Taylor   ISBN 0 948003 84 7

Exploring otherness (PF24)
An approach to cultural awareness
Barry Jones   ISBN 1 874016 42 9

Broadening the learning experience

New contexts for modern language learning (PF27)
Cross-curricular approaches
Kim Brown & Margot Brown   ISBN 1 874016 50 X

With a song in my scheme of work (PF25)
Steven Fawkes   ISBN 1 874016 45 3

Drama in the languages classroom (PF19)
Judith Hamilton & Anne McLeod   ISBN 1 874016 07 0

Being Creative (PF10)
Barry Jones   ISBN 0 948003 99 5

All Pathfinders are available through good book suppliers or direct from **Grantham Book Services**,
Isaac Newton Way, Alma Park Industrial Estate, Grantham, Lincs NG31 9SD.
Fax orders to: 01476 541 061. Credit card orders: 01476 541 080

Pathfinder 32

A CILT series for language teachers

Foreign Language Assistants

A guide to good practice

*David Rowles, Marian Carty
and Anneli McLachlan*

CiLT

Centre for Information
on Language Teaching and Research

The views expressed in this publication are the authors' and do not necessarily represent those of CILT.

The authors would like to thank Anthony Howick, Head of the Foreign Language Assistants Department at the Central Bureau for his help and encouragement during the preparation of this book. Also John Thorogood for his cartoons on pages 51, 52, 54, 55 and 59 and Pat McLagan for her contributions on pp47–49.

Finally many thanks to all our colleagues — teachers, pupils, advisers, and of course, FLAs.

First published 1998
Copyright © 1998 Centre for Information on Language Teaching and Research
ISBN 1 874016 95 X

A catalogue record for this book is available from the British Library
Printed in Great Britain by Copyprint UK Ltd

Published by the Centre for Information on Language Teaching and Research,
20 Bedfordbury, Covent Garden, London WC2N 4LB

CILT Publications are available from: Grantham Book Services, Isaac Newton Way, Alma Park Industrial Estate, Grantham, Lincs NG31 8SD. Tel: 01476 541 080. Fax: 01476 541 061. Book trade representation (UK and Ireland): Broadcast Book Services, 24 De Montfort Road, London SW16 1LZ. Tel: 0181 677 5129.

Contents

1. Introduction

The potential contribution of the Foreign Language Assistant (FLA) to the learning of a foreign language in schools is immense. In a recent survey carried out on behalf of an Advisory Group on FLAs set up by the DfEE and the Central Bureau (Summer 1997) over 99% of the schools responding stated that FLAs were a valuable resource, and a number of them highlighted the extreme frustration caused by severe budgetary constraints which had prevented them from currently benefiting from the services of an FLA. Nevertheless, FLAs continue to support the work of language departments in over 4,000 schools and colleges throughout the UK.

The FLA's unique contribution has been clearly recognised over a long period of time but has been even more fully appreciated since the introduction of the National Curriculum. As pointed out in a leaflet produced by the Central Bureau, FLAs offer invaluable support to **learners** by:

- providing an opportunity to hear a young native speaker, thereby stimulating genuine classroom communication;
- assisting the teacher in the classroom or working with small groups of pupils away from the classroom;
- enabling more pupils to take part in individual conversations in the foreign language;
- bringing, by their very presence, the foreign country and its culture into the classroom.

They also help the **modern languages department** by:

- providing invaluable oral practice for both teaching and testing;
- acting as a model speaker to facilitate classroom demonstrations;
- sharing in the task of assessing pupils' progress;
- producing authentic materials for use in the classroom;
- bringing printed and recorded materials from their own country;
- being available as a constant source of INSET and professional development for staff.

The vital role that FLAs can play is perhaps best summarised in *Modern languages for ages 11 to 16* (DES, 1990):

> *Above all, FLAs help to reinforce the essential message to both teachers and pupils of the central importance of the use of the target language in the classroom, a principle which is fundamental to our proposals (for the National Curriculum). Pupils need to feel that they can communicate effectively with a native speaker in the target language . . .*

Moreover, many of the statutory requirements of the Programmes of Study are best met by skilful and judicious deployment of FLAs, who have a particularly helpful contribution to make in the implementation of the often much neglected Programme of Study Part 1. This highlights the areas of:

- Communicating in the target language;
- Language skills;
- Language learning skills and knowledge of language;
- Cultural awareness.

The authenticity of the FLA's language and their very presence in the school is invariably seen to raise the profile of language learning and the work of the department in the school as a whole. For the pupils, whether through timetabled lessons or via social or informal contact, the chance to be involved with a youthful assistant does much to increase motivation. The FLA also provides invaluable support by keeping teachers up to date on more obscure idioms and neologisms and on current social and political trends in their native land.

 ## MAXIMISING THE POTENTIAL

Despite the enormous advantages that having FLAs as part of the modern languages team can bring, there is some evidence that schools, their pupils and the FLAs themselves do not always derive as much benefit as they might. There are a number of pre-requisites to be considered to ensure that the FLA's presence in the school is fully effective and there is a general consensus that their contribution to a school is greatly enhanced when:

- there is a **clear departmental policy** or strategy as to how to make the best use of the FLA's presence;

- there is **consistency of approach** within the department;

- despite pressure of time and other demands, opportunities are created for inducting the FLA and offering **continuing support and guidance;**

- **problems** sometimes associated with the obligation of sharing FLAs with another school, e.g. timetabling restrictions and conflicting advice, are **openly addressed and resolved;**

- busy heads of department do not become complacent with regard to the Assistant scheme — they acknowledge its importance and the need to retain their enthusiasm **for restarting the training process with a new FLA every year;**

- individual teachers within the department are prepared to welcome the FLA into their own classroom and, where appropriate, are willing to change their style in order to **incorporate fully the FLA into the lesson;**

- sufficient time and thought are given by all teachers to **planning activities** FLAs might undertake with small groups and last minute arrangements are avoided;

- FLAs are not put in the difficult position of having either **too much or too little freedom** to decide upon their programme of activities;

- **FLAs themselves are ready to adapt to their role,** develop appropriate interpersonal skills, remain committed to their work, show initiative and resilience and are willing to work hard to motivate their groups while nevertheless having realistic expectations of their learners.

Most departments find that any initial difficulties with individual FLAs can usually be rectified as the year progresses. FLAs bring many strengths, such as:

- youth, vitality, a number of common interests with their pupils,especially in the sixth form;
- a natural and current model of their native language;
- an up-to-date perspective on their own culture;
- a curiosity about and interest in the country where they are appointed;
- an eagerness to become involved.

But they are also likely to be vulnerable in a number of different areas. It is more than likely that they will have:

- no teacher training experience nor even perhaps that of leading groups of young people;
- little or no first hand experience of the culture and approaches of UK schools;
- no experience of having taught their own language and no real appreciation of the difficulties encountered by pupils attempting to learn their language;
- no realistic awareness of appropriate standards of achievement for pupils at different levels and stages;
- a lack of familiarity with the demands of GCSE and 'A' level examinations;
- uncertainty as to what appropriate 'management' language to use, how to deal with unmotivated or disaffected pupils, what sanctions are available, etc.

It is therefore essential, if the partnership between schools and FLAs is really to achieve its full potential and ensure that maximum achievement and personal satisfaction are gained, that time and commitment are given by all those involved.

This Pathfinder is based upon examples of good practice drawn from a wide range of schools. It aims to facilitate the task of the department and the FLA in working successfully together.

It offers ideas on organisation, deployment, planning, preparation and monitoring and suggestions on how to develop the FLA's role as a support in the classroom as well as working with smaller groups. There are references to such key issues as group management, pupil motivation and catering for different levels of ability. There are also specific sections devoted to GCSE and 'A' level examinations — areas where, research has indicated, FLAs spend the majority of their time. There is also a discussion of strategies which support the successful delivery of a range of communicative activities and the part played by language games. There is a recurring emphasis on the motivational role of the FLA — pupils like and need to feel that learning languages with the FLA is different and is fun — but there also needs to be structure and a sense of progression.

The book has been divided into two sections. Part 1 contains a general review of opportunities and responsibilities in relation to both the department and the FLA. It is intended to be read by all members of the modern languages team including, naturally, the FLA. In this way it should be possible to ensure a consistent approach across the whole department to ensure that the FLA's contribution is fully effective.

Part 2 consists mainly of practical guidance and advice for the FLA. It contains a number of specific examples of activities and approaches which have proved to be successful. Although this section will be of primary interest to FLAs, and is addressed directly to them, it could also provide helpful suggestions for teachers when considering the role which they wish the FLA to undertake with their pupils.

The book is quite deliberately and specifically geared to the FLA's pedagogic role and responsibilities. It makes no reference to personal and social aspects beyond the school nor to various administrative issues which sometimes exercise FLAs. These are important matters but are very fully dealt with in the Central Bureau circulars *Notes for FLAs* (SD/N100) and *Notes for schools and colleges receiving FLAs* (SD/N101).

THE UNIQUE CONTRIBUTION OF THE FLA

The FLA:

- provides a real and meaningful context for pupils to practise communicative language skills;

- offers an up-to-date model of his or her own language;

- satisfies the native speaker element required by the National curriculum;

- can give a clear insight into culture and current affairs in his or her own country;

- ensures, by his or her presence, a variety of approach which is different from other lessons given by the language department;

- can be asked to recommend and provide a wide range of authentic materials and help support visits and exchanges to his or her own country

- can, if encouraged to do so, be an effective means of INSET for staff and help develop teachers' language skills;

- is generally close to pupils in terms of age and interests and is therefore a strong motivating force;

- brings a different perspective and a different personality each year and represents a range of different regions and countries;

- at the current rate of salary, undoubtedly represents very good value for money.

C*i*LT

Part 1

2.   The department's role

 HOW TO BEGIN

The modern foreign languages department provides an FLA with the focus for his or her new experience. The first few days are crucial in ensuring a successful year for all and must be carefully planned to ensure maximum success with minimum disruption for busy teachers. A mentor should be named for each FLA. This may be the head of department or head of the language in question. But consideration should also be given to younger teachers. They will be nearer the FLA's own age and perhaps more likely to share in his or her experiences, as well as having fewer administrative tasks. Acting as a mentor is also a useful professional development opportunity in terms of management skills.

The mentor should draw up a programme of guided classroom observation so that the FLA becomes familiar with the workings of the department and all its members in the shortest possible time. Specific areas for the FLA to consider during the period of observation might include the following:

1   **Noting the importance of the target language, paying heed to commonly used target language instructions and observing the consistency with which they are adhered to:**
   - How often does the teacher use English and why?
   - What are the main commands in the target language the teacher uses?
   - How much target language do the pupils use?

2   **Considering the use of visual or textual aids to support meaning:**
   - How are flashcards used?
   - What other visual support is provided?
   - What is the role of the written word during oral work?

3   **Observing questioning techniques:**
   - What sort of questions require a yes or no answer?
   - How does the teacher use either/or questions?
   - Is there a structured way to get to the correct answer?
   - How does the teacher praise pupils?
   - How does the teacher decide which pupil should answer the question?
   - Are pupils encouraged to ask questions as well as answer them?
   - How does the teacher correct wrong answers?

4 Observing repetition techniques:
- What different techniques does the teacher use to vary repetition?
- How much time needs to be devoted to this aspect of teaching/learning?

5 Observing the relationship between teachers and pupils:
- How does the teacher ensure good relationships?
- How does the teacher warn a pupil?
- How does the teacher deal with difficult pupils to ensure minimum disruption?

6 Studying strategies used to motivate reluctant learners:
- How does the teacher keep pupils on task?
- What kind of activities, materials, approaches achieve the best results?

7 Considering the role of grammar:
- How often does the teacher discuss grammar?
- How much English does the teacher use when talking about grammar?
- How many technical terms does the teacher use when talking about grammar?
- Are they different from the terms the FLA uses?

8 Observing how experienced teachers pace a lesson:
- How often does the teacher change the activity?
- What kind of different activities or pupil groupings are used?
- Do pupils work together in pairs or groups within the classroom?
- For what kind of activities?
- For how long?
- How are the activities set up?
- How does the teacher consolidate the language learned?

9 General structure of the lesson:
- How does the teacher introduce the lesson and also draw it to a conclusion?
- When introducing new activities what kind of instructions or explanation does the teacher give?
- Are examples always given of what type of response is required by the teacher or by other pupils?

A planned programme of observation invariably involves FLAs within the lesson and it is natural that they should be introduced to each new class at the earliest opportunity. Teachers must be aware, however, of the **need for FLAs to observe the teacher and class in action** in order to judge the tenor and style of a particular department. It is also important that FLAs do not perceive their role solely as impromptu information providers, where no preparation is called for.

Observation might last for up to two weeks, in order for a wide range of classes to be seen. The FLAs should play an increasingly participative role in the classroom as they gain in confidence and understanding.

The observation process must be exploited through a thorough debriefing of the FLA by the mentor on a regular basis. Debriefing is the key to a successful induction programme. The mentor should take the FLA through an overall impression of their observation, reinforce the culture of the British classroom and pay particular attention to the school's ethos. Many FLAs are shocked by what they perceive to be a lack of grammar in language teaching in the UK or a high level of indiscipline. These issues are better tackled from the outset, rather than left unsaid.

The following are **useful debriefing questions,** prior to a more detailed discussion of some of the points listed earlier on pp5–6:

- What surprised you most during your observations?
- What impressed you most?
- What did you think about the pace of the lesson? The pupils' level of attainment? Relationships within the class? The variety of activities? The teacher's and the pupils' use of the target language?
- Which aspects of what you have seen do you feel confident about being able to deliver yourself?
- Which aspects do you think will be quite difficult?

HOW TO ENSURE CONSISTENCY WITHIN THE DEPARTMENT

Modern foreign language teachers naturally have individual styles and approaches, but each member of the department has a responsibility and a duty to deploy the FLA appropriately and effectively during his or her lessons. Individuality should not mask inconsistency, professionalism must come before personalities. It is the responsibility of the mentor, in conjunction with the head of department, to ensure that individual teachers are playing their part. Job descriptions for the FLA stating clearly what is expected of them should be drafted to serve as a regular reminder to all concerned.

Soon after the FLA's arrival, he or she should be invited to a departmental meeting. This is where the head of department outlines respective duties for all parties, making reference to the departmental handbook. Thereafter, FLAs might be invited to meetings as appropriate, for example, when work is being moderated or oral examinations are being discussed.

Consistency is best achieved through clarity. The mentor should explain basic principles, how to keep a register, how to set out lesson plans, how best to record what has been done and how to give feedback to both students and teaching colleagues in line with departmental policy. The mentor should establish a ten-minute weekly debriefing slot where the FLA can touch base and discuss any outstanding successes or nascent problems.

HOW TO FACILITATE JOINT PREPARATION AND PLANNING

Joint preparation and planning is the key to a successful partnership. However, modern language teachers are very busy people; preparation must therefore be swift, but effective. If an FLA is clear about tasks from the outset, he or she will be able to work with a greater degree of autonomy.The mentor should ensure that the FLA has access to relevant sections of the departmental handbook and departmental schemes of work, textbooks, examination syllabuses and other resources.

All parties are best served if an FLA knows exactly where to look for particular materials. The mentor must, however, guard against plunging the FLA into a morass of paperwork and National Curriculum jargon. This can only be counter-productive. It is incumbent on the FLA and all teachers whose pupils are taught by the FLA to timetable in a regular planning slot. This need not be lengthy, but must be adhered to for the sake of good practice. Clear instructions are essential, particularly in the first few months. FLAs frequently do not understand how closely one has to stick to a particular structure or a given field of vocabulary to ensure it is absorbed effectively. The first departmental meeting with the FLAs could be used to show how closely a scheme of work is followed.

Departments might wish to consider writing the role of the FLA into their scheme of work on an ongoing basis. If annually reviewed, good practice can be developed from one year to another.

ESTABLISHING EXPECTATIONS AND OFFERING PROPER SUPPORT

The busy first few weeks will set the pattern for the year. Clear expectations as outlined above will aid induction and ensure smooth operation for the rest of the year. The mentor is the first port of call, but all members of the department have a responsibility for the FLA's well-being and state of mind. The FLA should be left in no doubt that he or she will receive the full support of the school's discipline procedures in case of rudeness or abuse or poor punctuality. Referring disciplinary problems to the mentor or the head of department should be seen as a sign of strength and commitment rather than weakness.

The department should take great pains to ensure that the FLA is introduced to colleagues from other departments and encouraged to play an active part in extra-curricular and social activities. This will provide FLAs with additional opportunities for improving their English, as well as meeting a broader range of people and combating what could be for many, especially at the beginning, a somewhat lonely existence. If they are able to establish a number of social contacts where they can practise their English, FLAs may be more ready, at least on some occasions, to speak to language teachers in the target language — an opportunity which teachers should not dismiss lightly.

FLAs are usually particularly appreciative of invitations to join outings and school visits, as well as being invited to teachers' homes, especially during the early stages when they are still finding their feet. Such hospitality is often richly rewarded by return invitations at a later stage to taste some authentic 'target cuisine' . . . However, FLAs should be aware of the fact, discovered by many of their predecessors, that in pressurised UK staffrooms it is often the FLAs themselves, in practice, who have to make the first move — and sometimes the second and third as well!

3.   The FLA's role

One of the principal elements of the FLA's role is to promote success and self-esteem. They have a very important part to play in bringing languages alive and in making sure that learning is fun. They have a traditional and inbuilt advantage in that the vast majority of pupils readily welcome the chance to spend time with the FLA and clamour to be nominated each time the opportunity arises. However, as has already been indicated, 'fun' does not come automatically and some careful planning and preparation is essential if the initial and instinctive level of pupil motivation is to be maintained.

The use of visual stimuli, textual support, games and other activities all require careful thought, planning and preparation time — especially in the early stages — and will be richly rewarded in the classroom.

Having spent an essential period of induction getting to understand how the school operates and how languages are taught, one of the key tasks the FLA must address is to find an appropriate level of language to use. It is advisable to start work with students at a very basic level, carefully controlling certain expressions which, although they may seem to be natural and straightforward to the FLA, could still be too sophisticated or idiomatic for pupils. FLAs should also bear in mind that the pupils will be accustomed mainly to the expressions, question forms and structures of their coursebooks — or of their teacher! — and may be perplexed by other linguistic forms, even though the latter may seem to be more appropriate as far as the FLA is concerned.

At various times grammatical questions may be raised by the students — or, it appears, quite often by the FLA whose language learning, both mother tongue and foreign, may well have been built upon a more overtly grammar based approach. While it is true that some students might benefit from grammatical discussions and explanations, FLAs should also remember that their pupils' knowledge of grammar may well be quite scant and that they may not use the same terminology as the FLA.

The speed of delivery and clarity of the FLA's language will be very important and it should be remembered that the use of mime and gesture is an essential adjunct in conveying meaning. The pupils are privileged in having an authentic model for producing speech patterns and the FLA should therefore ensure that pronunciation and intonation are of a high standard. Many British pupils are particularly careless in this aspect of learning and practice and the FLA is very well placed to try to raise standards. However, he or she must be wary of attempting to correct every single lapse which is likely to inhibit the pupil.

UK students will expect to establish friendly relationships with the FLA at an early stage and it is unquestionably true that they will work better with someone who shows apparent liking for them and is interested in them as individuals. Some previously appointed FLAs have raised questions about this domain, however, and have suggested that over familiarity at the outset may be an unwise path to follow. The FLA's status is closer to that of a member of the teaching staff than that of a student and they should ensure that an appropriate level of respect and, if need be, formality is retained. It is always easier to adopt a more relaxed style once a properly structured and controlled relationship has been established, rather than the other way round. This does not automatically mean that the FLA and students will not be on first name terms — a fairly common pattern in many schools — nor that the FLA should not use appropriate familiar forms of address (*tu, du,* etc) — in his or her own language.

A recent national survey (December 1997) of heads of department clearly highlighted a number of assets which were perceived to be priorities where schools' expectations or aspirations were concerned in relation to FLAs:

a) Knowledge and understanding
- familiarity with examination syllabi and test procedures;
- awareness of the National Curriculum and its principles;
- ability to help 'A' level students with their personal topics;
- capacity to inject life into GCSE role plays.

b) Personal initiative
- willingness to develop independence and take responsibility for planning;
- show resourcefulness in adapting to a variety of tasks;
- be active and energetic in creating materials.

c) Expectations and approaches
- not to set their expectations of pupils too high — this can be off-putting for students;
- need to value communication and confidence above accuracy;
- need to adapt to different levels of ability and pitch questions accordingly;
- be positive and encouraging;
- have clear expectations about discipline.

d) Techniques
- stay in the target language;
- speak sufficiently slowly and clearly;
- simplify language and restrict vocabulary and syntax;
- undertake regular assessment and record keeping.

e) General
- be enthusiastic about own language, culture and society.

The above list might appear to be quite daunting and certainly places a clear responsibility on schools to help FLAs to develop these traits, approaches and techniques. It is encouraging, however, to note how many FLAs are able to make a positive impact and, over the course of their stay, to fulfil many if not most of the expectations listed. One typical head of department put her view of the current FLA very succinctly: 'She is fab!'

WHAT THE FLA MIGHT EXPECT FROM THE PUPILS/STUDENTS

YEAR 7 AND YEAR 8 KS3

These pupils will probably be the greatest admirers of the FLA and the most overtly enthusiastic. As with the older pupils their enthusiasm will often outweigh their linguistic competence and accuracy. They are usually very keen to participate in active and drama based learning. Again, as with all the pupils, structured and visual support will be necessary to make the most of their enthusiasm.

YEAR 9 KS3

This is when adolescent inhibitions begin to set in and pupils are reluctant to show what they know. The FLA will need to build on to an even greater extent listening and reading skills to encourage speaking. He or she should aim gradually to build up pupils' confidence by setting them achievable tasks and readily offering praise. It should be borne in mind that at this stage of development many pupils find the coursebook — whatever it may be — to be 'boring' and the FLA will always benefit by offering a variety of 'different' activities.

YEARS 10 AND 11 GCSE

In the main these pupils are very keen to work with the FLA. In withdrawal situations they appreciate the more friendly atmosphere of the small group and the fact that the FLA is nearer their own age. The FLA can also add an extra dimension when working with the teacher in the classroom. The FLA must remember that UK pupils learning a foreign language have less curriculum time devoted to the subject by comparison with their European counterparts who learn English. Another disadvantage is the anglophone nature of global youth culture and, in particular, music. Unlike in the FLA's own country, our pupils have little exposure to music and media that is not English or American. In fact, for most pupils their sole contact with a foreign language and its culture will be the foreign languages classroom.

While some pupils will display confidence and enthusiasm, the FLA must be prepared for many to be 'tongue tied'. For some pupils the ability to **comprehend** — as opposed to **responding** in the target language — will be a significant achievement. As with the post-16 students, it is generally preferable to allow them to listen (and read) before expecting them to actually produce any foreign language. Part of the FLA's role is to compensate for the fact that our culture is monolingual, by providing the pupils with examples of music, magazines, video clips, etc.

YEAR 12 'A' LEVEL

These students will generally be committed to languages and well motivated. Their listening skills will be good and they will often be confident orally; however, their oral and written contributions will often not be grammatically accurate. At the beginning of Year 12 they may even produce writing that would be incomprehensible to a native speaker! Their reading skills, too, will be fairly limited. Their teachers will spend much of the first term 'revisiting' basic grammar and developing their discursive competence. The FLA's role will be to provide supportive, structured and enjoyable activities to sustain their enthusiasm for speaking while at the same time improving their grammatical accuracy.

Reading texts provide excellent support for speaking too. These should generally be short and concern topics of interest to the age group which allow them to express their opinions such as 'My ideal boy/girl friend,' personal relationships, family, and other broader issues such as the environment and future careers. It may, however, be necessary to keep the level of discussion at a fairly basic level since former FLAs have regularly made the point that UK students often do not have the linguistic tools nor a sufficient range of knowledge and ideas on topics of a 'political' nature to engage in a full debate. Simple poems and songs can be ideal starting points. The department may well have a structured 'A' level reading scheme in place to encourage and develop their skills in this area.

YEAR 13 'A' LEVEL

By this time 'A' level students are generally quite confident and the FLA will derive much enjoyment from working with them. He or she will be able to engage in more open-ended activities and students' reading and listening skills will have improved sufficiently for them to appreciate and enjoy more sophisticated authentic materials. The activities used in Year 12 can be recycled by providing language content that is more complex.

4. Deploying the FLA

 SHARING ARRANGEMENTS

In many instances, invariably because of limited budgets, FLAs have to be shared between schools. This practice is obviously regrettable because:

a) it inevitably limits the impact the FLA will have in an individual school and reduces the amount of FLA contact with individual pupils or groups of pupils (e.g. sharing often means that Year 7 and Year 8 do not have an opportunity to work with the FLA);

b) it adds an additional complexity in timetabling, supporting and monitoring the FLA; and

c) it means that the FLA will have less time to get to know a single school and its members of staff.

However, some FLAs interviewed at the end of their year have actually welcomed such a shared experience since it has given them a chance to have an insight into two different — and sometimes contrasting — examples of UK schools. Indeed, it has not been unknown to hear comments such as 'I am so glad that I spent half of my time in school A because if I had had to work only in school B . . .'

There is a range of different models for setting up sharing arrangements between schools. It is strongly recommended that a maximum two schools should be involved in such a partnership since, when this number has occasionally been exceeded, the difficulties listed above have automatically been exacerbated.

SHARING ARRANGEMENTS

	School A	School B
Model i)	Two days per week	Two days per week
Model ii)	Weeks 1, 3, 5, etc	Weeks 2, 4, 6, etc
Model iii)	Weeks 1, 2, 3	Weeks 4, 5, 6

(NB: most schools, even when sharing arrangements are necessary, try to arrange the FLA's timetable so that he or she has one free day per week — preferably a Friday or Monday to create an extended weekend and to provide some time for private study.)

Each system has a number of advantages and disadvantages:

MODEL I)

This is the most common approach and enables the FLA to maintain regular and frequent contact with each school and individual groups or classes. However, it also means that the range of classes and year groups that can be involved on those two particular days must be limited to, in most cases, six hours of FLA time. Therefore, some pupils will be prevented from working with the FLA. A degree of flexibility is sometimes possible, with schools arranging to swap specific days at, say, half-termly intervals. Such an arrangement, however, can be confusing for all concerned!

MODEL II)

This system ensures that the whole week's timetable is covered and it is possible for all classes to have access to the FLA, within the scope of the twelve-hour time allocation. (NB: it is occasionally necessary to remind FLAs — and also the department — that their commitment is for twelve **hours** not twelve **lessons** and that preparation time, as for all teachers, is expected to be undertaken as an additional activity. However, most FLAs are more than ready to put in extra time on occasions, since this is seen as a gesture of goodwill and often encourages schools to be flexible with regard to the FLA's departure and arrival dates at the beginning and end of term.) The provision of a separate week timetable obviously creates a longer gap between meeting individual students or groups and does not suit those schools operating eight- or ten-day timetables.

MODEL III)

This approach is comparatively rare but has been known to work effectively where FLAs are involved with FL2 or FL3 and/or schools wish to use them for intensive sessions.

 ## TARGETING SPECIFIC GROUPS

Two very early decisions face the department when considering how to deploy the FLA:

i) Which pupils should have access to the FLA?
ii) Should the FLA operate mainly as an in-class support or with withdrawal groups?

In responding to the first question most schools give priority to 'A' level students, followed by those preparing for GCSE. This is a logical reaction since the FLA will clearly be able to help students to prepare for those examinations, the level of the students' foreign language — particularly in the sixth form — should make for more meaningful exchanges and dialogues, and the relatively small age difference means that a number of common interests are likely.

For most 'A' level students the session with the FLA is in addition to any timetabled lessons with the teacher and is geared to a whole 40–50-minute period, since this length of time is usually an appropriate match to the students' interest and ability levels. Shorter sessions might suit less confident students. However, there will also be occasions when it is particularly relevant for the FLA to participate in a normal sixth form class lesson, supporting the teacher, for example, in the introduction of a new topic.

While FLAs are almost always pleased to be working with sixth formers, many have expressed serious reservations at what they are asked to do to help GCSE students. The single most common complaint from them at the end of their year has been the sheer drudgery and monotony of practising role play situations and preparing stilted 'general conversations', which are tedious both for the FLA and for students. Clearly if work of this nature is to be part of the FLA's input, imaginative approaches to the task must be sought and ways explored to bring the FLA's cultural background into play. Suggestions on possible approaches are discussed in Part 2.

The boredom and frustration experienced by some FLAs when dealing with certain GCSE tasks is usually countered by their pleasure in working with beginners whose limited knowledge of the foreign language is more than balanced by their sheer enthusiasm for the subject and their interest in making contact with a native speaker and someone from a different cultural background.This should be borne in mind when drawing up the FLA's timetable and efforts made to involve younger pupils, at least during certain times in the course of the school year, to give a further boost to their motivation.

It has also been observed that there is an equal opportunities issue associated with the deployment of FLAs. If they are timetabled to work exclusively with the most able students — i.e. those who, by the very nature of their studies, are more likely to travel abroad — then a large proportion of pupils will be deprived of making contact with someone from a different cultural background. An opportunity for combating prejudice will therefore be lost.

However, it is not sufficient just to stand an FLA in front of a particular group and assume that cultural differences will automatically dissolve. A specific and structured programme needs to be devised if this option is to succeed and it may depend on the specific skills and interests of an FLA in any given year (see Chapter 8, p35).

A final choice in this area concerns the most desirable frequency of contact:

- Should pupils from a Year 10 class, for example, be withdrawn from the language class in groups of six to eight for the whole lesson, thereby ensuring that they have a substantial session with the FLA but possibly only on a monthly basis?

- Should each group have perhaps three or four consecutive sessions over a two or three week period, allowing them to build up some sort of a rapport with the FLA and some sense of continuity, but then having little further contact for the remainder of the year?

- Should the intention be to send three or four different groups to the FLA during the lesson for perhaps ten to fifteen minutes?

- Should individual pupils be given five-minute 'bursts', enabling many members of the class to have regular access and to replicate in some sense the oral examination?

The idea of short, sharp sessions is not generally rated very highly. Most schools and FLAs favour a system which allows for perhaps a minimum of twenty minutes with a group of about four to six pupils. They also find that a whole 50-minute period may make heavy demands on the FLA's ingenuity and the pupils' concentration. It is also worth noting that both FLAs and students find that operating on a one to one level on a regular basis can be very demanding for both parties — even at sixth form level.

Whatever arrangement is finally opted for, two other considerations arise:

a) **The need for the teacher to plan carefully the content of the lesson** from which pupils are being withdrawn so that time is not lost but also so that the groups are not disadvantaged by their absence. Some teachers see this as a good opportunity for a period of silent but monitored reading — an important but often neglected attainment target — or for a major session involving IT. Alternatively they may set up a series of 'carousel' activities, one of which is a session with the FLA.

b) **The opportunity to work as a group member with the FLA should be considered a privilege** and any semblance of disruptive activities should be reported to the teacher and carry the threat of the privilege being withdrawn.

WORKING ALONGSIDE THE TEACHER IN THE CLASSROOM

There are a number of advantages if the FLA is utilised as a support teacher within the classroom:

a) The trained, experienced teacher has prime responsibility for the structure and management of the lesson.

b) The FLA can observe at first hand how the teacher deals with such matters as motivation, organisation, discipline, etc and take note of questioning and correction techniques for future reference.

c) The FLA can develop a better understanding of pupil needs and appropriate levels of attainment.

d) By its very nature a shared lesson should involve a certain amount of pre-planning to establish a structure and the respective parts to be played by FLA and teacher.

e) The use of the target language is more authentic and easier to sustain.

f) Dialogues, role plays and discussions can be conducted in a more natural and meaningful manner and can be geared to introducing new structures.

g) More effective use can be made of pair and group work — the presence of the FLA, in effect, halves the class size.

h) The contribution and effectiveness of the FLA can be readily recognised by the teacher and further advice and guidance will be based upon having actually seen the FLA in operation.

i) The lesson is a distinct entity, involving the whole class. There is no need for special planning to allow for the absence of certain pupils working as a withdrawal group with the FLA (see above).

The majority of teachers invite the FLA into their classroom for a lesson or two at the beginning of their appointment, encouraging pupils to question him or her about personal background and interests. Other ways in which FLAs and teachers can operate productively in tandem on a longer term basis include the following:

Operating in tandem

- adopting a number of fictional or real identities;
- introducing new vocabulary and structures by means of joint presentation and repetition;
- acting out dialogues together;
- making encouraging comments in support of each other while working;
- repeating/rephrasing (in a varied manner) so as to reinforce what the other is saying;
- joining in demonstrations — two can provide a greater scope and also seem more realistic;
- encouraging the pupils to watch, in turn, the FLA or teacher — keeping them on the ball;
- one person providing visual support or gestures while the other is giving a description or explanation;
- pinpointing or writing key words on the board or OHP;
- organising the class into pairs or small groups with FLA and the teacher taking responsibility for different groups;
- ensuring all pupils are involved;
- checking pupils' comprehension — individually or in groups;
- reinforcing praise;
- encouraging pupils to ask for help and responding speedily to their needs;
- correcting individuals' mistakes discreetly;
- ensuring that pupils stay on task during group- or pairwork activities and maintaining constant supervision;
- sustaining the overall pace and variety of the lesson by giving each other occasional 'breathers';
- having the FLA teach the majority of the class while the teacher conducts oral assessments with a small group in one corner;
- supporting and supervising individual reading activities — helping with difficult vocabulary, explaining structures and cultural contexts, asking questions on the text, etc.

Further examples of good practice are given in the Central Bureau's video production *Working together* and the accompanying notes for guidance.

Why, then, with so many benefits clearly identified, is the team teaching approach still comparatively rare as a regular and sustained activity, according to feedback from FLAs at the end of their year?

There appear to be several reasons:

a) For this system to work well, good and reasonably detailed planning is essential. As has already been stated, teachers do not always have — or are unable to make available — the necessary time for planning.

b) A degree of imagination is required to ensure that both participants are fully and productively involved — FLAs have sometimes spoken of their minimal role in team teaching and complained of being merely a 'living dictionary', sitting on the sidelines.

c) A number of teachers are very much geared to the autonomy of their own classroom and find it difficult to share that role or be comfortable if another adult is present.

d) Some teachers, particularly those not teaching their first foreign language, are reluctant to use the target language in front of a native speaker.

e) FLAs may feel more comfortable in a withdrawal situation, where they can dictate the pace and nature of activities and where they can establish a different sort of relationship with their pupils.

In practice many schools find that a balanced approach is often most effective, with the FLAs spending up to half of their time working alongside the teacher throughout the year and not just as an induction activity. A combination of lessons built around a well thought-out set of activities, while for the rest of the time the FLA works independently with individuals or small groups, works well. In this way the FLA is conscious of a sense of personal development and increased confidence but remains in regular contact with the appropriate syllabus and coursebooks and can constantly pick up new ideas and techniques.

WITHDRAWAL SESSIONS

These sessions should not be considered to be an 'easy option', involving less time in preparation and planning. A number of basic questions must be applied to this style of working:

a) Has the right balance been struck by giving the FLA **helpful guidance rather than the teacher being too prescriptive?** One of the most common sources of irritation expressed by FLAs is to be told two minutes before the lesson what they are expected to do with a particular group.

b) How does the work the FLA will be doing fit into the **overall programme for this term/ year?**

c) Are the **accommodation and resources** available to the FLA appropriate and adequate?

d) How can the teacher obtain **feedback on the quality of the FLA's work** and the progress and attitude of the pupils? In particular, it is important to ensure that the FLA is **persevering in using the target language** with withdrawal groups, as many find it very tempting to lapse into English at the first sign of pupil reluctance to attempt to understand or speak the foreign language.

e) Has the FLA been asked to maintain a **general record of the topics covered,** structures practised and some indication of individual performance?

f) Has the FLA been persuaded too easily by the pupils to allow the lessons to be dominated by **games activities of limited value** such as Hangman or endless Word Searches?

Further advice on the management of groups is contained in Chapter 6 and in Part 2 of this Pathfinder.

SOME OTHER THOUGHTS . . .

Many FLAs will spend much more time than their allotted twelve hours helping out a department or specific individuals but a clear, formalised timetable from the outset is absolutely essential.

The FLA's cultural knowledge and handwritten script should be used to enhance notices and display within the department.

Creativity should be encouraged but preparation should not be seen as burdensome by the FLA.

Personalities can play an enormous part in how best to deploy FLAs, depending on their confidence and temperament, and the mentor's early judgement on this issue will be crucial.

5. The FLA and examination classes

 ### GOOD PRACTICE AT SIXTH FORM LEVEL

Integration of the FLA at 'A' level is a comparatively painless process. He or she has an invaluable function as a source of opinions, facts, examples and as an agent of vocabulary enrichment, paraphrasing and providing synonyms. **The presence of an assistant in a lesson introducing a new topic is a great help** to teachers and students alike.

Grammar can pose a problem at 'A' level. Teachers should share their philosophy regarding grammar with FLAs, but the bulk of grammar teaching should lie with the class teacher for the sake of clarity.

PREPARATION FOR THE ORAL EXAM

The 'A' level oral exam differs according to exam board. Task types invariably include the following:

a) interpreting;
b) reacting to a stimulus, e.g. an opinion poll or an advert;
c) preparing a presentation on a particular topic;
d) taking up a stance on a particular topic;
e) general conversation.

While the format of the exams may differ, oral skills are universal at 'A' level. Students need to be confident to express their views spontaneously on a variety of different topics. Memorised chunks of language are not acceptable. Many of the creative ideas suggested for GCSE students can be applied to 'A' level, but the FLA may choose to adopt a different approach, as the maturity level of the students will be considerably higher than for most GCSE students.

Interpreting: these tasks are most demanding, requiring a speedy response, a range of communication strategies and quick wits. Practice is the key to success here. The FLA should start small and work up to more complex scenarios.

Reacting to a stimulus: it is important for the FLA to provide authentic materials as a stimulus, a text or a picture which the students can refer to.

Topics at 'A' level include the following:		
Advertising	Health	Education
The media	Sport and pastimes	Law and order
The arts	Travel, transport and holidays	Politics
Daily life	Social issues	Ethics
Food and drink	The environment	Technological advances

The FLA will need to work with the relevant teacher to decide which topic to cover and when. There are times, however, when the FLA may decide to use a topical reference and should feel free to do so. It is part of the FLA's role to keep the department and your students abreast of cultural and current affairs in his or her country of origin.

Sessions with 'A' level students are generally longer than those with younger students, and planning is therefore doubly important. 'A' level students will need the following support if they are to respond well to a task:

- vocabulary related to the text/picture;
- opinions!
- vocabulary to express their opinions.

The FLA may find that some British students have few opinions. It is important for him or her to encourage them to adopt a standpoint of some form. To provide vocabulary for the task in hand, the FLA could:

- provide a vocabulary sheet;
- brainstorm the vocabulary the students think they might need at the beginning of a session;
- highlight key words in the stimulus and suggest synonyms.

The FLA could also make a list of phrases for and against, phrases to balance opinions and general fillers in their own language for their students to use. FLAs will find that with regular attendance at their lessons, the pupils' powers of expression will increase enormously.

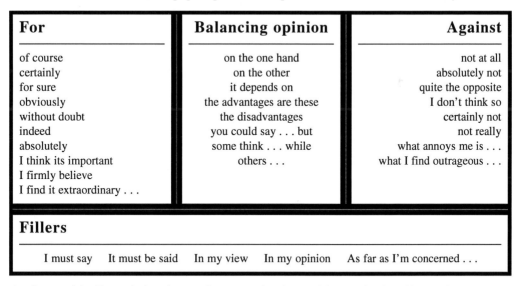

For	**Balancing opinion**	**Against**
of course	on the one hand	not at all
certainly	on the other	absolutely not
for sure	it depends on	quite the opposite
obviously	the advantages are these	I don't think so
without doubt	the disadvantages	certainly not
indeed	you could say . . . but	not really
absolutely	some think . . . while	what annoys me is . . .
I think its important	others . . .	what I find outrageous . . .
I firmly believe		
I find it extraordinary . . .		

Fillers

I must say   It must be said   In my view   In my opinion   As far as I'm concerned . . .

Again, as with all vocabulary items, these must be thoroughly practised and learned.

The above is intended as a guide only. The more diverse ways a student can express an idea, the better. The Mary Glasgow series *Advanced French/Spanish/German vocabulary* is a useful guide for the FLA, who should be encouraged to create his or her own file of exploitable materials.

FLAs need to acquire questioning techniques for exploiting texts and pictures. These are best learned via observation and this could usefully be included in the induction or observation programme. Sixth form level is ideal for the exploitation of authentic materials — songs, newspaper articles, poems. Departments should play to their FLA's strengths where possible. If an FLA is interested in art, music, cinema, sport or science, he or she should be encouraged to gather documents and create related tasks according to the level of student ability.

GENERAL CONVERSATION

It is useful to include at least five minutes' general conversation in every session. Students should be **encouraged to give and seek information** and should always be pushed towards analysis. Questions must be wide-ranging and open. The FLA should refer to current affairs and should try to cover all topics in the topic grid. One question leads to another. Students should be encouraged to think independently and pass from one subject to another. In this way, they will gain more marks for fluency.

Students should also be encouraged to find their own ways round difficulties. The FLA should resist providing them with an immediate solution straightaway and try to coax them round complex subjects, rather than offering them a way out immediately. Students need to be challenged to see if they can mount a counter-argument.

PREPARING A PRESENTATION

In this section of an exam, it is essential to guard against students choosing topics that are too broad. In the first instance, they should be advised on their presentations by their class teacher, but the FLA's work will be key in ensuring fine tuning and inclusion of local knowledge. An element of personal experience is important in the student's presentation — why they are interested in a particular topic, what is the motivation for their choice. The presentation must go beyond the narrative and the factual. It is the FLA's task to advise on research possibilities and to refine the structure. He or she should aim to act as 'devil's advocate' and to change the approach each time the presentation is practised. One very worthwhile additional skill to develop in the students is how to make notes in a foreign language

Relationships between FLAs and sixth formers are usually easy to develop because of shared interests but proximity in age can occasionally be problematic. FLAs should be open and friendly, but should not allow themselves to be diverted from the task in hand or taken for granted. As with any other year group, any difficulties should be referred to the mentor and the head of department.

GETTING STARTED IN THE SIXTH FORM

To give one instance of a possible approach, FLAs could start with their own personal biography which will involve the past, present and future tenses in an authentic and interesting way. The students can then listen to the same information for a second time and raise their hand when their own personal biography differs from theirs. This will allow them to listen to a 'model' which they can repeat, substituting their own personal details.

For example the FLA might say 'I started compulsory schooling at the age of six'. The students would put up their hands and say 'I started school at the age of four/five'. They then continue until they are 'interrupted' by the next difference. This can be followed by the students' oral presentations of their CVs which they can prepare in writing.

This activity is very useful in helping you to gauge the level of fluency and confidence of the students and to highlight any special difficulties they are experiencing with grammar, tenses, etc.

A POSSIBLE SCHEME OF OPERATION

One way of involving FLAs to good effect in the sixth form is to set up an intensive structured input. This is a system that operates at Elliott School, a mixed comprehensive school of 1,400 pupils in Wandsworth, where FLAs are used in the following way:

Sixth form students are grouped in pairs or threes and receive a timetabled weekly slot with an FLA, above and beyond their six 50-minute teaching periods per week. The FLA is charged with the task of improving oral skills, particularly with regard to reaction to a stimulus, development of students' chosen oral topics and general conversation.

At the beginning of Year 12, students learn how to analyse images and adverts, departing from the smallest utterance, adding detail, opinions and drawing conclusions. The FLA discusses with the class teacher the topic to be studied, in line with the work undertaken in class that term.

During every session five to ten minutes are devoted to open-ended general conversation. Students are encouraged to give reasons to support the answers they give and are continually encouraged to say why they think or do or say a certain thing. From the first term of Year 12 onwards they are taught to justify their opinions.

After the spring half term, students consider their choice of oral topic, discussing it with their class teacher, the FLA and their partner. They then set about their research, drawing up five areas of interest within their chosen topic. For example, if the topic were the Media, the areas of interest might be: television; advertising; the press; use of images; women in the Media. At this point, the arrangement for grouping is fairly flexible as it may be more profitable for one student to have a slot alone with the FLA from time to time. Once the framework is established, the normal course of lessons is resumed, with the FLA working henceforth from stimuli, including general conversation and asking sixth formers questions on their chosen topics. As the Year 12 exam approaches, students are given a mock exam both by their teacher and the FLA.

In Year 13, the pattern continues, although the FLA, in conjunction with the teacher may choose to vary the stimulus, tackling longer texts, distributing these beforehand so that vocabulary can be checked and absorbed. Planning covers different language functions, mounting an argument, refuting suggestions, etc. FLAs are encouraged to push the students to work to a higher register at all times. Towards Christmas mock exams are restaged. The oral component marks at Elliott have risen substantially as a result of this intensive structured input.

THE FLA AND GCSE

As noted previously, how an FLA is deployed will vary to some extent depending on individual departments. What is virtually certain, however, is that, unless employed in a sixth form college or an FE Institution, the FLA will be expected to work with pupils to prepare their GCSE oral examination. While the focus will be on encouraging pupils to speak, the FLA needs to remember to use listening, reading and writing activities to support the speaking tasks.

The FLA will need to be clear that there are three different types of exam, all of which comprise a listening, speaking, reading and writing element:

1 a terminal exam which requires pupils to prepare for an exam in all four attainment targets at the end of the two-year course;

2 a terminal exam plus coursework;

3 a modular exam which requires pupils to complete assessment tasks periodically during the two-year GCSE preparation time, all of which count towards the final assessment.

Topics throughout the course will be based upon the five Areas of Experience highlighted in the National Curriculum:

• everyday activities;
• personal and social life;
• the world around us;
• the world of work;
• the international world.

When FLAs arrive in school they should be provided with the GCSE syllabus which contains all the information required concerning the examination

From summer 1998 the oral exam will comprise two sections:

Section (i)   role play
Section (ii)   a presentation and discussion and a general conversation

Tasks are provided at **foundation** and **higher** levels which the head of department should describe in greater detail. It should also be possible to supply the FLA with sample tapes produced by the examination board and advice and guidance concerning the mark scheme.

The following list is typical of advice given by schools to their sixth formers and GCSE students and should serve as a helpful introduction to FLAs:

HINTS *for preparing conversation*

1   Remember that every question implies several more. Say as much as you can about anything connected with the question, e.g. Have you any brothers and sisters (how many? names? ages? schools/places of work/ appearance?) This will help you to score highly in **content** and **independence.** Try to give at least three facts in any reply.

2   Simplify things you cannot translate easily, e.g. if your relative is an air traffic controller say he or she works at London Airport . . .

3   If you understand the question, but do not know how to express the true answer, be prepared to be 'economical with the truth' — the important thing is to keep going in order to get good marks for **fluency** . . . and the examination board will not check up on your answers!

4   If you find something difficult to explain, don't stutter and stumble — say so! 'That is really very complicated/It's difficult to explain/I haven't a clue/I can't remember/I can't recall exactly when . . . where . . . who', etc.

5   The examiner will avoid asking many questions which only require 'yes/no' answers. When one arises, however, try to address the examiner as *madame, senor, signorina,* etc and introduce extra phrases such as: yes — certainly, undoubtedly, hopefully, absolutely, in fact or no — not at all, on the contrary, unfortunately, not really, I hope not, etc.

6   If you do not understand a question, say so — in the target language — and ask for it to be repeated — perhaps more slowly.

7   Learn as many synonyms as you can. They are very useful when you are asked several questions of the same type. This is especially true when you are asked to express an opinion — 'I quite like, I adore, I'm fairly easy about, I enjoy, I don't like, I loathe, I am not bothered, I couldn't care less', etc.

8   Prepare what you can say on each topic. Use the syllabus to give you ideas on what you might be asked and write down some key words when you are practising.

9   Learn 'link' words to improve your marks for fluency: 'sometimes, normally, often, never, from time to time, every month, every Monday', etc. Learn expressions of time: 'the first morning of my stay, once, another day, one weekend, on the last evening', etc.

10   Learn as many expressions as you can for giving your opinion.

THE FLA AND ASSESSMENT

It is inappropriate for FLAs to conduct formal assessments and assign examination type grades, since they are often not clear about levels of performance. They can play a full and productive part in preparing students for ongoing assessment opportunities and exams. FLAs play a key role in practising areas of experience, vocabulary and structures learned in class, bringing it all together in a meaningful way. An extra body and a new pair of ears allow the student to refine their powers of expression, bringing authenticity to the dialogue. While the FLA should not be expected to conduct examinations, he or she is perfectly placed to mock up an exam scenario for practice purposes.

It is useful for the department to agree on a feedback policy for oral work. GCSE, GNVQ and 'A' level syllabuses all operate fairly complex mark schemes. Depending on the level, departments might adopt a policy of requiring feedback from their FLAs on the students' oral performance. A simple 1–3 scale of assessment might be implemented:

1 = very good, 2 = fair, 3 = poor.

If such a scale is deemed to be useful, the teacher should induct the FLA thoroughly so far as expectation levels are concerned.

Departments could encourage FLAs to write comments in their registers. FLAs and students alike respond well to feedback and need to know that their time has been well spent.

Grammatical accuracy can pose a problem at foundation level. FLAs must be made aware of communicative teaching methods and could usefully discuss with their mentors what constitutes a sympathetic native speaker.

6. Organisation, teaching strategies, accommodation, resources

 ## PLANNING THE SESSIONS

In the best scenarios the FLA will plan collaboratively and in advance with the class teacher or head of department. This will ensure that the work is integrated rather than bolt on. The FLA should be aware of the linguistic objectives via the schemes of work and exam syllabuses and ideally will have worked out with the class teacher the activities and resources to be used.

The FLA should be equipped with visual, textual and auditory support in each session. The visuals will include flashcards provided with coursebooks as well as those drawn by the FLA. Simple drawing will suffice and publications such as *Cartoons for classroom communication* and *1,000 pictures to copy* are invaluable to both teacher and FLA.

GROUND RULES

From the outset the FLA should establish a number of clear organisational ground rules which will apply to all groups but probably less rigidly with sixth formers. He or she needs to consider the following questions:

How should the pupils address the FLA?
- Informal or formal register.
- *Monsieur /Mademoiselle, Fraulein/Herr, Senor/Senorita.*
- First name.

How will the FLA address the pupils?
- 11–14-year-olds.
- 14–19-year-olds.

How should pupils respond to questions or stimuli in lessons given by the FLA?
- Individuals put hands up.
- Via pairwork.
- Chorus response.
- Series of individual responses.
- Wait for the FLA to indicate who responds next.

How will the FLA involve all members of the group?
- Plan 'listen and do' activities as 'warm ups' (see Part 2).
- Brainstorm previously learned language.
- Encourage them to volunteer rather than pick on an individual.
  (NB: but ensure that **all** pupils participate — at least to some degree — and also that no individual dominates the lesson)
- Plan pairwork to allow pupils to practise in a stress free environment.

USING THE TARGET LANGUAGE

As native speakers FLAs are an invaluable human resource. They can convey to pupils that their language is as valid a language for communication as English by sticking to it in the classroom. They should also use their language to some extent outside the classroom as well as during lessons, e.g. greetings, talking about the weather. However, for social reasons or to find out more about pupils and their personal background and interests, the FLA will obviously want to speak English.

Target language: guidelines for FLAs

1 Persevere! Speak in the target language whenever possible, even if some of your pupils reply in English.

2 Keep it simple. Try to speak at normal speed but clearly.

3 Be theatrical! Support what you say with gesture and or visual support.

4 Include your **management language** ('Sit down, open your books, show me, put your hand up', etc) in your planning of the session.

5 If pupils don't understand — paraphrase or use one of the more confident pupils as an interpreter.

6 Establish 'contracts' with lower ability pupils whereby the target language is used exclusively for short periods of the lesson, e.g. 'For the next ten minutes I am going to talk only in French/German/Spanish and you must try to understand all you can'.

WORKING WITH GROUPS

Working on his or her own with small groups of pupils will allow the FLA to create a relaxed, informal yet intensive working atmosphere. It is likely that the groups will be decided by the class teacher. They can be organised in a number of different ways:

- random;
- friendship;
- ability;
- mixed-ability;
- gender.

The size of groups will vary, but to facilitate pairwork, the FLA should try to ensure that groups are comprised of even numbers.

LEARNING THEIR NAMES

In Key Stages 3 and 4 FLAs are unlikely to see pupils every week so they need to make a conscious effort to learn the pupils' names and find out about them. This process can be begun during the period of observation. Use of names is not only vital for classroom management and discipline purposes, but also makes the pupils feel valued and shows that the FLA cares about them. Knowing the pupils' names is also an essential aspect of differentiation (see Part 2 for further details).

INTEREST LEVELS

There will be a difference in terms of the interest that pupils bring to sessions which will affect their motivation and in turn their ability to learn. The **content** of what is taught must take account of the National Curriculum and GCSE, but will need to be as broad as possible to retain the interest and involvement of pupils. It is therefore important that the **activities** which are prepared for pupils to learn the GCSE content are both challenging and within their reach. As with learning styles, motivation levels are not inherent but elastic! Motivation comes from active, personal involvement. 'Ability' will also play a part but ability is not static either and can be enhanced by the activities a teacher or FLA uses and the degree of success achieved by the pupils.

QUESTIONING TECHNIQUES

FLAs need to study carefully the various questioning techniques that the teachers use. In very broad terms, questions for most pupils at the level of Key Stages 3 and 4 will be of the 'who? what? where? when?' nature, i.e. usually of an essentially factual nature — whereas with more able GCSE pupils and sixth formers they will be centred around 'how? why? and why not?' issues, demanding a higher level of interpretation and response. In the early stages FLAs should concentrate on structuring questions at three different levels, depending on how new the language is and how able and/or confident the pupils are, e.g.:

a) is it an x?   (the level of individual comprehension will dictate
b) is it an x or a y?   in which order these questions are asked)
c) what is it?

DIFFERENTIATION

It is important to bear in mind that all the pupils the FLAs encounter will have different learning styles. The FLA, as a teacher, will need to respect these individual differences yet at the same time encourage pupils to extend and use a variety of techniques.

Learning styles can be divided into Visual, Auditory and Kinesthetic. Learners with a predominantly visual learning style will rely on pictures and text, those with auditory awareness will rely on sound, kinesthetic learners will use movement to help themselves learn. Research has indicated that most learners — of whatever age! — retain information and knowledge as follows:

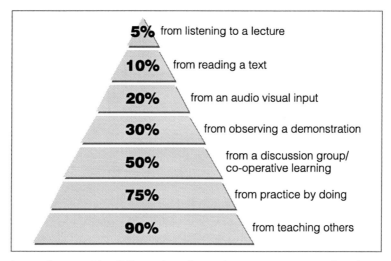

5%	from listening to a lecture
10%	from reading a text
20%	from an audio visual input
30%	from observing a demonstration
50%	from a discussion group/co-operative learning
75%	from practice by doing
90%	from teaching others

Apart from the need to consider different learning styles, any one group of students, even at 'A' level, could contain individuals with a wide range of **differing ability and motivation.** The FLA therefore needs to plan and be prepared for **different:**

- levels of response;
- tasks in relation to a a single text (audio/written);
- amounts of time required by pupils to complete tasks;
- texts on the same topic;
- attention spans.

Strategies to support learning in these circumstances include:

- extension work;
- an element of choice;
- reference sheets;
- pairwork — matching pupils by ability or contrasting ability.

DEALING WITH ERROR

Errors should be dealt with sympathetically. It is important that pupils say, or at least hear, the correct version of the language but it is equally important that this is done sensitively. Repeated correction of individual pupils can be counterproductive and may embarrass them or stop the flow of language. It is often better to focus the attention of the whole group on errors and correct them collectively at the end of an exercise.

GAMES

Games provide pupils with a real purpose for using their language and should be used with **all** levels of learner. The content will vary according to the linguistic competence of the group.

Why use games?

- They provide a fun element.

- They allow pupils to use the language for real purposes.

- They develop collaborative skills such as taking turns and listening to others in competitive games the desire to win motivates many pupils.

- They create a relaxed atmosphere.

- They can allow pupils to be physically active in a controlled way.

- They allow pupils to work independently of the FLA.

- They allow the FLA to monitor pronunciation and accuracy in non-threatening way.

- They allow pupils to work at their own pace

- By varying the language content many games can be recycled.

There are many excellent publications on language games. Investigation within any department will reveal a wide range of games with which the pupils are familiar. FLAs should build up their own repertoire from the period of observation onwards, while teachers should suggest games as and when appropriate. One tool which is particularly useful for assistants — and recyclable for departments — is the board game.

A simple classroom language game can lead on to much more complex activities. Questions on a board game can range from: 'What's your favourite colour?' to 'Why are people racist?' The possibilities are endless. Taking the activity one stage further, students can work together with assistants to produce the materials.

 ## ACCOMMODATION

The FLA should be provided with **a room suitable for the purposes of teaching.** Working in corridors, stock cupboards, under stairwells or even in dining halls demeans the work and status of the FLA and is often distracting for the students. Whenever possible the FLA should be timetabled in a small group room or the departmental office. Where providing suitable accommodation is a real problem schools should consider using the FLA more extensively in a team teaching role.

If possible the FLA, perhaps in conjunction with a fellow FLA, should take some responsibility for the display in the room where his or her lessons take place. This should convey some form of ethos reflecting their own country. It could comprise of brochures and posters but might also include a range of realia, public notices, references to topics currently being studied, etc.

Arranging the room in advance will convey to the pupils that the FLA is organised and in charge of what happens in the classroom.

Use of resources and equipment

In order to fulfil his or her duties, an FLA should have regular access to the following equipment: cassette recorder, video recorder and overhead projector. An FLA should make active use of this equipment and not simply rely on his or her language skills to get by.

How to use these items

Cassette recorders may be used to record the FLA, alone or with others, or simply to play an audiocassette of a song, a text to be worked on, perhaps a jingle. Transcriptions of the texts used are very helpful after the task has been completed. The recorders can also be used to record students and to indicate the progress they have made as well as pointing out — gently and selectively — any major errors or mispronunciations.

Video recorders provide the FLA with an invaluable resource. A video player facilitates the full exploitation of colourful pictures — images always help the learner — and the use of a wide range of questioning techniques.

Students can:

- be asked to predict what will happen next in a particular sequence;
- watch the picture without the text and can imagine what the commentary would be;
- listen to the commentary without the picture and can say what they think the image shows.

Overhead projectors are excellent tools for gathering brainstormed material. It is a good idea to group vocabulary according to different colours. OHPs can be used for building up role plays and dialogues, with students suggesting different possibilities and the FLA throwing in unpredictable elements. Using pictures, FLAs can build on basic vocabulary input, playing guessing games, revealing part of a picture, encouraging pupils to speculate as to what it might be. Pupils can move on to give their own opinions of different activities. FLAs can overlay text to support learning and tenses can be changed while using the same materials. Such pictures also provide a good source of games.

A video camera, if available, can be highly motivating. It can be used to film role plays, individual interviews with students, short playlets, sixth form discussions, etc. Many FLAs have taken the initiative to make a short promotional film about the school or locality, helping students to produce a commentary in the target language.This may be one of the occasions when it is advantageous for the FLA to work with pupils off-site. However, it must be clearly stressed to them that there are quite specific routines and procedures to follow before such an activity can take place.

SUMMARY

Pace and variety are essential for effective learning to take place. The FLA has to have clear aims and objectives set out in small achievable steps. All contributions need to be valued and regular praise will have a motivating effect. Over-emphasis on recall should be avoided and language covered in previous sessions should always be revised. The FLA needs to have clear expectations in terms of behaviour and needs to be aware of the appropriate sanctions for infringements. Whole group sanctions or punishments are to be avoided at all costs. Pupils expect teachers and FLAs to behave fairly. When this does not happen, resentment grows and learning deteriorates. Any rewards system in operation should be made use of and there should be clear criteria for recognising effort and attainment.

7. Working to the four Attainment Targets

The National Curriculum has specified four Attainment Targets which should be given equal priority in modern foreign language learning.The four Attainment Targets are as follows:

AT1 — Listening and responding	AT2 — Speaking
AT3 — Reading and responding	AT4 — Writing

Although it is likely that FLAs will spend most of their time concentrating on ATs 1 and 2, they should not see these areas as being exclusive

Here are five ways in which FLAs can contribute to the development of the attainment targets across the department at all levels.

The FLA can . . .

Listening and responding

- play the unpredictable role in a role play situation with the class teacher;
- record tongue twisters and nursery rhymes for pupils to imitate;
- prepare listening discrimination exercises on gender and sounds;
- create an attitudes tape with phrases and intonation suggesting different frames of mind, e.g. anger, sympathy, gratitude;
- give a list of instructions for pupils to follow in order to draw or make something.

Speaking

- teach question forms on a particular topic;
- help pupils to make up rhythmic role plays, or a list of rhyming words on a particular topic;
- teach filler phrases and idiomatic phrases to keep a conversation going;
- provide a model answer for pupils to adapt on a particular topic;
- take part in a class survey answering all pupils questions in turn.

Reading and responding

- write simple target language definitions of difficult words to help pupils get started on a text;
- teach pupils to identify key words within a magazine article;
- read agony aunt letters and discuss the content;
- read short stories and poems together;
- look at different sorts of magazines/ newspapers with students to compare the differences.

Writing

- contribute to a class brainstorming session as a preparatory writing activity;
- work with pupils to redraft a piece of writing on a particular topic to improve the quality of the language;
- write simple summaries of course reading books to guide pupils in their choice;
- write an imaginary diary after your arrival in this country giving pupils your everyday experiences and feelings;
- make a checklist of the most common avoidable grammatical mistakes.

8. The cultural dimension

 PROGRAMME OF STUDY

The National Curriculum underlines the importance of developing cultural awareness as part of the modern foreign languages programme. Section 4 of Part 1 of the Programme of Study, as well as stressing the need for linking teaching to authentic materials, highlights four aspects of cultural awareness where the FLA clearly has the potential to play a major role. It states that pupils should be given the opportunity to:

4b come into contact with native speakers in this country;

4c consider their own culture and compare it with the cultures of the countries . . . where the target language is spoken

4d identify with the experiences and perspectives of people in those countries;

4e recognise cultural attitudes . . . and learn the use of social conventions.

The SCAA publication *Modern foreign languages in the National Curriculum — managing the Programme of study Part 1* gives a few examples of ways in which FLAs can become involved in raising cultural awareness. This includes the following, which could be conducted in varying styles with pupils of different levels of linguistic ability and maturity:

4b carry out conversation with the FLA (all levels);

4c learn about other countries where the foreign language is spoken — their culture, food, religions, festivals, history, geography;
  - listen to speakers of the foreign language talking about their everyday lives in familiar/ unfamiliar contexts;
  - compare uniform, school life, leisure, singers, shopping;
  - take part in European Awareness days (which could be prepared jointly by a group of FLAs at one or several schools);
  - discuss the rights and responsibilities of pupils of the same age;
  - discuss politics;
  - read teenage magazines (together);
  - discuss similarities and differences.

4d talk about festivals and customs;
  - discuss the classroom environment;
  - contribute to display;
  - compare daily routines;
  - use video materials presenting foreign countries and peoples to stimulate discussion;
  - FLA talks about life in own country — describes (own) interests, lifestyle. food, etc;

4e use of various forms of address — familiar and formal greetings, ways of thanking, shaking hands, kissing!
- learn system of names, how to address envelopes, ways of expressing appreciation, proverbs and similes, etiquette and protocol, body language;
- learn formalities in letter writing;
- learn about birth, marriage, death;
- study broadsheets/tabloids (together) and compare different styles of media reporting and importance of local/regional newspapers.

AREAS OF EXPERIENCE

Part 2 of the Programme of Study also provides a whole range of opportunities for FLAs to play a role in developing cultural awareness via the listed Areas of Experience:

A Everyday activities, including
- the language of the classroom;
- home life and school;
- food, health and fitness.

B Personal and social life, including
- self, family and personal relationships;
- free time and social activities;
- holidays and special occasions.

C The world around us, including
- home town and local area;
- the natural and made environment;
- people, places and customs.

D The world of work, including
- further education and training;
- careers and employment;
- language and communication in the workplace.

E The international world, including
- tourism at home and abroad;
- life in other countries and communities;
- world events and issues.

CULTURAL AWARENESS PROGRAMME

A selection of the above headings could provide the basis for an extended cultural awareness programme for the FLA or a form of checklist to ensure that the pupils actually do broaden their awareness and understanding of another culture. This is not always the case — many FLAs have reported that their cultural input was haphazard, purely coincidental, unplanned and often merely in relation to (sometimes outdated) textbooks.

A 'cultural awareness programme' might either be part of the department's handbook or notes of guidance for FLAs. It could also be freshly drawn up and mutually agreed between department and FLA every year, depending on the particular strengths and interests of the FLA. The FLA will need to be advised that each of the agreed areas can be revisited at different levels. This will depend on the pupils' level of comprehension and expression, ranging from simple information giving where beginners are concerned and much fuller discussions and comparability exercises when working with sixth formers.

In planning and implementing this aspect of their work FLAs must be fully aware of the following points:

- one of the chief aims for teaching languages to all pupils is to break down national and regional stereotypes and to combat racism. They should be aware that elements of the British press have a tradition of reinforcing stereotypes and of creating hostile attitudes to foreigners. The pupils therefore may have a totally caricatured or unrepresentative picture of the FLA's country and its inhabitants.They should also be encouraged to talk about different regions and their characteristics both within their own country and beyond — where appropriate — where their language or culture has established itself, such as North Africa or South America;

- it is important to resist the temptation to concentrate too extensively on the 'quaintness' of certain cultural aspects. Efforts should be made to underline cultural similarities as well as differences;

- FLAs need to be aware that many of our pupils — even in the sixth form — may be less politically and culturally aware (or even interested) than their counterparts in the FLA's own country. FLAs should not make too many assumptions about their pupils' knowledge or readiness to discuss general issues;

- music, films and books which are not firmly rooted in an anglo-saxon background and origin have rarely established themselves as favourites in the minds of UK teenagers. Many FLAs have been disappointed that their own cherished pop or folk music has made so little an impression on their students (with the historical exception of *Joe le Taxi* . . .)

- wherever possible the FLA should try to maintain the principle of conveying the essential information and explanations in the **target language,** whatever the protestations of the group. However, on occasions the reality of the situation may dictate that:

  - pupils will need particular training in questioning skills and preparation, before a topic is introduced. This may require some elements of vocabulary being explained if they are going to be able to cope with a presentation in the target language.

  - occasionally, the FLA will decide that the topic is of particular importance/interest and will feel that the use of English is merited. However, if at all possible, this 'concession' should be restricted to certain sections of the lesson such as the beginning or end.

INCORPORATING THE CULTURAL DIMENSION — WAYS AND MEANS

- Straightforward presentation by FLAs on different aspects of their personal background.

- Role play performances of national figures, different professions, etc in their own country.

- FLA questions pupils about their own culture, interests, activities, etc as a starting point to understanding and appreciating other cultures.

- FLA and pupils work together on data collection/project preparation related to specific cultural aspects (shopping habits/leisure activities/ attitudes to TV programmes, etc).

- Collection of newspapers and magazines (sent regularly from home) to conduct ongoing survey of local news stories (current events, sports results, media personalities, etc), with a view to comparing different approaches and priorities.

- Joint FLA/pupil compilation of 'A day in the life of . . . (a pupil, a teacher, a policeman, a mayor, a shop assistant, etc)' as perceived in the two countries.

- Using maps and historical perceptions to obtain comparative perspectives (different treatment of Waterloo, Dunkirk, Joan of Arc, etc).

- Discussing not only habits and customs but also attitudes (e.g. to family, food, TV).

- Watching TV excerpts (news, game shows, adverts etc to compare approaches).

- Cooking and experimenting, making artifacts and models, following printed instructions.

- Drawing up town plans based in different countries.

SETTING UP LINKS AND CONTACTS

Although they naturally provide a living breathing example of their own culture FLAs must guard against being seen as the 'typical' French/German/Spanish/. . . person. FLAs must, instead, recall other people and experiences from their own background to convey and explain different viewpoints. However, it is likely that the more they personalise their culture, i.e. by referring to **their** favourite club, showing photos of **their** family or house, describing how **they** spend their Sundays, the greater will be the impact on their pupils.

FLAs also have a role to play in providing a direct link to their own country. This could be done in several ways:

- setting up and overseeing a link with their own secondary school back home (exchanges of letters — often better as a group activity — audiotapes, videotapes, contact via fax, e-mail, etc). It is very important to control language levels in these activities and to ensure that the information exchange is of a simple nature if the pupils are involved with individual contacts;

- helping in the setting up in their home country of a work placement scheme and preparing students for this experience;

- preparing pupils for a day trip or residential visit to their country and accompanying the visit.

9. Reviewing the FLA's contribution

It is important for the mentor to set aside quality time to review and evaluate the FLA's work. Ideally this should be done on a termly basis, but it is especially important to carry out such an exercise at the end of the first term.

The following questions could be used as a framework for this review

1   The pupils
- How are the pupils responding?
- Do they attend as scheduled?
- Do they behave appropriately?
- Do they respond positively to the FLAs cultural 'inputs' such as songs, articles, photos, video recordings, poems?
- Do they enjoy the sessions?
- Do they understand?
- Do they speak?

2   The FLA
- Does the FLA stick to the target language?
- If not, how can the FLA be helped to do this?
- Are the necessary materials and resources easily accessible?
- Is the FLA confident with what he or she is being asked to do?
- Does the FLA need help with planning?
- Is the FLA receiving enough support from all members of the department?
- Does the FLA feel integrated into the wider life of the school?
- Is the teaching accommodation suitable?

3   The colleagues in the department
- Do colleagues let the FLA know well in advance what they want him or her to do?
- Do they use the FLA effectively alongside them in the classroom?
- Are pupils of all abilities given access to the FLA?
- Do they respond promptly to any discipline problems experienced by the FLA?

4   The wider staff perspective
- Has the FLA been introduced and his or her role explained to the administrative and secretarial staff?
- Are the senior management aware of the FLA's work and supportive of it?
- Are staff generally welcoming and prepared to show interest in the FLA?

Part 2

This section is geared particularly to the needs of FLAs and is therefore addressed directly to them. It offers practical guidance and advice on both organisation and teaching techniques and also suggests a number of specific learning activities. However, although it is anticipated that FLAs will appreciate the suggestions made as being especially appropriate to their role, other members of the MFL department may well find that many of the tasks and ideas proposed are also very relevant to their own practice.

When applying ideas from this section to the classroom itself the FLA should, however, bear in mind the following recommendations:

a) there is a substantial amount of material contained in this section. To avoid confusion, it might be preferable to concentrate on one activity at a time, to try the same approach with different groups, to learn from the experience and make any necessary adaptations and improvements — rather than trying to introduce several activities at a stroke;

b) although the majority of the suggested activities are aimed at motivating and helping GCSE pupils — since this has constantly been identified by schools and FLAs as the area of greatest need — they can be readily adapted to the needs of other students, particularly in the sixth form. This can be achieved by changing the structures, adding different tenses, altering the context etc. Many suggested activities can also be used with younger pupils by retaining the principles of the activity but simplifying the language demands.

NB: all of the examples given in this section are in English so that the guide can be readily adapted to the needs of all FLAs, regardless of their native language and country of origin.

10. General guidance for the FLA

 ## GETTING TO KNOW THE PUPILS

Learning pupils' names as soon as possible is an important pre-requisite for effective dialogues between you and them and this task should be given priority attention. One way of approaching the task is as follows:

Prepare name cards for all the pupils taught.

P P P P P P

P   **P**

FLA

Arranging the room in a semi-circle or horseshoe to ensure eye contact can be made with all the pupils, you then devise a seating plan

Place your prepared name cards where you want them to sit.

As they enter, greet them by name and shake hands (cultural awareness).

Address them by name when asking them to contribute or when praising them for responding to your questions or stimuli.

Use their names when taking low-key action in response to minor infringements of classroom rules (not listening or looking out the window, talking quietly, etc).

 ## GETTING STARTED

PRACTISING THE SPECIFIC LINGUISTIC STRUCTURES

Pupils need to spend time listening intensively before being expected to produce language.

You will have specific linguistic objectives in mind. These would normally be at the practice rather than presentation stage of learning, i.e. the pupils will have already encountered the language in question and are needing to consolidate it in a range of different situations. The following format might help.

'WARM-UPS'

These will be based on language that your pupils are **very** familiar with. Pupils listen and respond.

Stand up   if you like . . . / you have a . . . / your favourite _____ is . . .
      you have been to . . . / you don't . . . , etc.

Put yourselves into groups . . . according to the colour of your shoes, your hair, your eyes, if your birthday is in the same month, etc.

PUPIL TO PUPIL LANGUAGE

Here you will provide pupils with the opportunity to interact with one another by 'controlling' each other.

Divide the group into partner 1 and partner 2. Partner 1 tells partner 2 when to start, when to stop, to speak louder, softer, more quickly, more slowly. Partner 2 chants the alphabet/numbers days of the week/months of the year according to his or her partner's 'orders'. They then swap roles.

LISTEN AND RESPOND

Using visual stimuli (with textual support) make a statement. The pupils respond with YES/NO or TRUE/FALSE.

REPETITION AND VARIETY

In order to make language theirs, pupils need to hear and use the language on many occasions. However, if the repetition is tedious and predictable, boredom will set in. Bored pupils don't learn effectively. At best they become passive and at worst disruptive.

Some repetition techniques:

1 **Varying the volume.** According to the teacher's or a pupil volunteer's instructions the group repeats loudly (so that Mr X can hear) or very quietly in a whisper.

2 **Varying the speed.** According to the teacher's or a pupil volunteer's instructions the group repeats very slowly, a bit faster, very fast.

3 **Saying something a certain number of times,** e.g. 'During the holidays I went to the cinema with my friends' five times.

4 **Saying something with a certain emotion,** e.g. with joy, sadness, disappointment, anger, boredom, anxiety, etc.

5 **Saying something like a famous 'person',** i.e. Donald Duck or the Queen.

6   **Breaking up sentences.** Divide the group into parts of the sentence.

Pupils 1 and 4	Pupils 2 and 5	Pupils 3 and 6
Where	did you go	during the holidays?

Teacher counts to three and pupil 1 begins. As the pupils say their 'part' they stand and sit when finished, the next 'part' stands, says his or her words, sits and so on.

7   **Against the clock.** Either in groups or as individuals (volunteers). Pupils say the sentence. The fastest time is the winner.

8   **Setting the phrases to a round** (Frère Jacques, London's Burning).

9   **Moving a pointer** quickly around a set of visuals and the language is repeated.

10   **True/False.** Pupils repeat the language if correct — shout wrong if not, etc.

11   **Spelling words.**

12   **Spelling words** in the air with your finger.

13   **Mouthing words** and pupils guess what is being said.

14   **Mimes.** You say phrases, pupils carry out appropriate mimes — or vice versa. In pairs, partner 1 mimes, partner 2 copies the mime and says the phrase.

15   **Like a train picking up speed:**

I went	five times slowly
to the cinema	five times faster
with my friends	five times faster still
on Saturday	five times very fast
night	once like drawn out like a whistle

16   **As a rap,** rhythmically.

17   **As an opera singer**

18   **Spot the deliberate mistake.** Place a familiar text (the current role play) on OHP. You read the text but you make deliberate mistakes. Pupils shout 'stop' at the appropriate point and provide the correct version.

19   **Sequencing.** A role play or dialogue is cut into OHT strips and placed on the OHP in the wrong order. Pupils read and then tell you to put the strips in the correct order. Using the following language (which you provide if necessary):

The first sentence is . . .	The next one is . . .
Then it's . . .	After that . . .
Then it's . . . , etc.	Finally it's . . .

20 Throwing a ball. With the text (role play) displayed on the OHP you start and throw the ball to a pupil who must say the next line/part, that pupil then throws the ball to someone else (and so on) until the text has been read.

21 Blocking out the text. Text is displayed on the OHP. You gradually block out the text. The group reads in chorus repeatedly until the entire text is blocked out.

22 *Chef d'orchestre.* Text is displayed on the OHP and the lines numbered. A volunteer will be sent out of the room. The rest of the group chooses a *chef d'orchestre*. The *chef d'orchestre* will guide the group reading through the text via a specific gesture such as folding her arms, scratching her head, removing her spectacles, etc. The group repeats the first line until the *chef* makes her gesture. Each time she makes the gesture the group reads the next line down.

The volunteer returns to the classroom and tries to find out who is the '*chef d'orchestre*' by observing closely the moves and gestures of the group.

PRACTISING BY DOING: LEARNING ABOUT YOUR PUPILS

Modern Foreign Language lessons abound with opportunities for you to get to know your learners.

USING GRIDS TO COLLECT INFORMATION

When pupils are being questioned on the topic of *Families and pets,* make a note about each pupil using a grid like the one below.

name	brother	sister	pets	birthday

Once your grid is complete, you can 'test' your pupils on how much they know about each other, e.g. 'Who has one sister, no brothers and a hamster and has a birthday on 6 June?' You are providing them with a real purpose for questioning them in the first place and you are then using the information that you have collected.

FIND SOMEONE WHO . . .

Prepare a list of instructions (according to their linguistic level) which will enable your pupils to ask simple questions.

Practise the questions first:

Do you have . . ?   Do you like . . ?   Have you been to . . ?
What is your . . ?   What's the name of . . ?

The pupils circulate and ask the questions of different members of the group. They must make a note of responses to report back to you.

Find someone who . . .   has cat/sister/brother
                           likes chocolate/maths/French/German/Spanish
                           has a _____ in his/her bedroom
                           has been to _____
                           has the same   *favourite TV programme*   as you
                                            favourite pop group
                                            favourite colour
                                            star sign
                           knows the name of the French/German/Spanish/Irish/Belgian prime
                           minister

11. Using authentic materials

You may have been asked to bring 'authentic materials' from your home country to add to or update the department's existing collection and to provide resource stimuli for your own lessons. Items requested by departments often include the following:

- up-to-date books — including reference books;
- magazines of interest to teenagers;
- copies of regional/national newspapers;
- timetables and tickets;
- tourist office brochures;
- menus;
- postcards — preferably with accompanying handwritten text;
- personal photographs, including family, friends, pets, locality, etc;
- personal documents — identity card, driving licence, etc;
- personal school reports and other school documentation;
- official forms which have to be completed for e.g. passports, travel passes;
- supermarket and hypermarket publicity sheets;
- taped songs;
- children's rhymes;
- simple poems;
- simple games;
- posters;
- mail order catalogues.

All of the above, if appropriately used, could undoubtedly be supportive elements in creating language learning situations and as 'cultural' indicators. However, you should be aware that many of your predecessors have sometimes struggled to import trunk loads of materials, much of which has been barely used by either teachers or FLAs! There are two guiding principles to observe before embarking on major stockpiling:

- always consult very carefully with the Head of Languages **in advance** to establish the key requirements;
- try to envisage exactly **how you might be able to use** the materials you intend to bring with you;

It is perhaps worth bearing in mind that many FLAs are able to bring back from their homeland extra materials after the Christmas break, by which time they are much more aware of what resources would be helpful.

ci**LT**

Activities you can prepare
in relation to authentic materials

1 Write target language questions. These can range from questions needing a yes or no answer, through multiple choice questions to questions that are wholly open-ended.

2 Write true or false questions on a particular timetable/menu/bus ticket — or ask your pupils to ask such questions.

3 Use symbols to help pupils understand meaning. Ask them to put the symbols in order, or to say which ones do not appear in the text.

4 Write gapped texts based on the materials brought.

5 Cut the texts up, so that they have to be put in order.

6 Write headlines to summarise paragraphs. Ask students to put the headlines in order.

7 Compare one particular piece of realia with its British equivalent. Highlight cultural differences.

8 Make up a 'missing person' bag full of realia, creating a life, e.g. bus timetable, identity card, telephone number, etc. Ask students to recreate the person's life orally.

9 Use cartoons to teach pupils to look carefully at pictures. Teach the vocabulary specifically for a particular cartoon.

10 Use photographs of yourself and your home to provide model answers for them to talk about their own lives.

Your work as a FLA is likely to be most successful if the resources and materials used:

- stimulate the pupils' imagination;
- include interesting, humorous and dramatic pictures and objects;
- include elements of surprise and drama;
- provide opportunities to discuss current events and culture.

So called 'authentic' materials, i.e. those which have not been produced for the purpose of foreign language teaching and learning — can be ideal for motivating pupils. Some possible strategies for you to employ and adapt are listed below:

PHOTOS, PICTURES AND POSTCARDS

These should be preferably unusual, bold, coloured. You can teach language such as ' it could be . . . I think it is . . . it seems to be . . .' Ask 'Why do you think that?' frequently in response to pupils' statements. Below is a list of possible activities:

Memory game — show the image for one minute, then hide it and ask for actions and objects remembered.

Twenty questions — silhouette a picture of a famous person an an OHP transparency. Give clues to identify him or her and answer pupils' questions.

Pupils fill in empty speech bubbles and invent captions for cartoons and pictures.

In someone else's shoes — pupils describe the likely feelings and reactions of a person portrayed in a particular situation or incident.

Pupils question you on your personal photos (family, pets, home town) or postcards and brochures of your local area.

Words on a postcard are used for the basis of a **description of a whole holiday** to the rest of the group.

 ## TV, VIDEO AND RADIO

These provide authenticity, language in context and cultural elements. The most commonly used clips are short news items, weather reports, adverts, documentaries (related to teenage interests), soap operas and dramatic parts of films. Also popular are videos of interviews and discussions between you and friends and your relatives, illustrating holidays, activities, the local area, and so on. Try the following:

Brainstorm likely vocabulary before showing the clip and note it on the OHP/board. Check out the language as pupils watch/listen.

Prediction — show a short extract and ask: 'What is it about?', 'What do you think will happen?', 'Who will appear?' Pupils could discuss it in pairs and report back.

Show the clip without sound and ask the pupils to provide key words or describe what is happening.

Play the clip with sound but no picture. Pupils say what is happening, where it takes place and suggest a description of the individuals involved, giving reasons for their choices.

Pupils respond to: 'Tick/put your hand up when you hear . . .'

Devise a viewing/listening grid with key questions such as: Who? What? When? Where? How?

PRINTED MATERIALS

Use newspaper articles (especially *faits divers*) supported by a pre-reading activity. Sort the key nouns/verbs beforehand and distribute them to pupils who try to construct the story before comparing it to the original version.

An alternative version to the above: you hold a cutting of an incident or event in your home town and pupils must gradually piece the story together by questioning you. For example: 'Where did the incident take place?' or 'How many people were involved?', etc. Subsequently other students can take over your role with other cuttings. This is an excellent means of improving students' questioning skills.

Present a human interest story containing many quotes. Pupils work in pairs to reconstruct the interview using the quotes to help them.

In someone else's shoes — pupils imagine their feelings if they were involved in a situation/incident reported in the newspaper.

Jigsaw reading — cut a newspaper article into sections and give each pupil a different section. Individual pupils summarise their section and the group puts the story in the correct order.

Use a collection of realia items (brochures, tickets, menus) to suggest a sequence of events. Pupils use them as clues and piece together the mystery story.

What's in the bag? — collect items likely to belong to a teenager. Pupils must guess each object and then suggest a description. Items are taken out singly for recognition and later replaced in the bag for a memory test.

Pariscope, etc — arrange outings, times, meeting points, and make travel arrangements.

TV listings — discuss and compare programmes, describe types of programme and express preferences.

Pupils complete blank forms (passport, post office, social security, etc) possibly with bogus identity which has to be guessed by rest of the group.

12. GCSE activities: preparation for the oral examination

 ROLE PLAY

Here are some two examples of role plays. Each is followed by possible activities. A role play works in the following way:

ROLE PLAY 1

The scene is set: You are staying with a pen friend.
You do not feel well.
The candidate has pictures to prompt him or her.

FLA	What is the matter?/ Are you unwell?
pupil	*I don't feel very well, I have a headache and a temperature.*
FLA	Oh dear, can I get you anything?
pupil	*Yes , a cup of tea/a hot drink.*
FLA	Of course/OK.
pupil	*I am going to bed now.*
FLA	OK.

It is useful to establish the final dialogue so that you know what you are working towards. The pupils need to be familiar with both roles in order to complete the role play successfully.

One straightforward way of varying role play practice is to ask one of the participants to adopt a particular attitude or frame of mind — they are tired, bored, angry, particularly happy, etc. You might give the lead in this activity with the pupils subsequently conveying their own chosen mood, having observed your performance. This way of approaching role play can be further enhanced if the dialogues are recorded on audiocassette or video.

An alternative strategy is to insist that one of the elements of the dialogue should be unknown, thereby introducing an element of unpredictability (Would you like to eat later on? How long do you want to rest?) which the pupil must either invent or respond to.

Activity 1: *Pelmanism/pairs*

Prepare text cards with questions, ailments and remedies on coloured card.

(i) Questions	**(ii) Ailments**	**(iii) Remedies**
What is the matter?	I have a headache.	May I have some paracetamol/aspirin?
Oh dear! Can I get you something?	I have stomach ache.	May I have some paracetamol/aspirin?
	I have a period pain.	May I have a cup of tea/ a hot drink?
	I have a backache.	May I have a drink of water/ a cold drink?
	I have a sore throat.	May I have a cup of tea/ a hot drink?
	I have a sore knee.	May I have some cream?
	I have cut my finger.	May I have a bandage?
	I have cut my knee.	May I have a bandage?
NB: *You will need enough remedies to match up with the ailments!*	I have been bitten by a mosquito.	May I have some cream?
	I have a temperature.	May I lie down/go to bed/ go for a rest?

Prepare corresponding cards with visuals on different coloured card, e.g.

Task (i) in pairs/ individually/ in groups of three or four:

- The pupils lay out their text and visual cards face down in rows.
- In turn each pupil selects two cards, one of each colour.
- One pupil must read the text card out loud.

- Statements linked to the visual should also be attempted either by this pupil or his/her partner(s).
- If the text card corresponds to the visual card the pupil keeps the cards.
- If not they are returned to the rows face down.
- The next pupil takes his or her turn.
- The game continues until all the cards have been selected and kept by one of the pair.
- The winner is the one who has the most pairs.

Task (ii)

This works along the same principles, only this time the pupils have to match the remedies to the ailments. It can be done first with the text cards and then with the visuals. They can now practise the whole dialogue.

Activity 2: visuals

Write the dialogue out on an OHT, copy it onto another OHT and cut it into strips (this could also be done using a piece of A3 paper and card). Copy the dialogue several times onto card and cut it up. Place the card strips in envelopes. Prepare enough for your group to work in pairs.

Display the dialogue **with visuals** on an OHP:

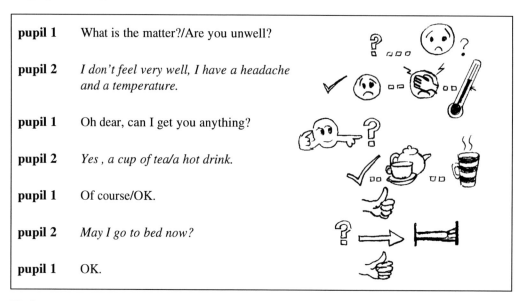

pupil 1	What is the matter?/Are you unwell?
pupil 2	*I don't feel very well, I have a headache and a temperature.*
pupil 1	Oh dear, can I get you anything?
pupil 2	*Yes , a cup of tea/a hot drink.*
pupil 1	Of course/OK.
pupil 2	*May I go to bed now?*
pupil 1	OK.

Task

- Divide the group into two — **pupil 1 and pupil 2**, count to three and ask them to read the text in their groups. Swap roles so that the whole group has practised both roles.

- Set up the group in pairs and distribute the envelopes with the strips of card. Demonstrate using the OHP that they have to put the strips in the correct order. Give them a time limit, the first pair to finish are the winners.

ROLE PLAY 2

The scene is set: You are buying food for a picnic at the campsite shop.
The candidate has textual cues to prompt him or her.
The dialogue they need to prepare will go something like this.

Shopkeeper (FLA)	Good morning/afternoon. Can I help you?
Pupil	*Yes I would like some apples.*
Shopkeeper (FLA)	How many would you like?
Pupil	*I would like a kilo please. I would also like some strawberries.*
Shopkeeper (FLA)	I am sorry, there are no strawberries left.
Pupil	*Never mind, I would also like a bottle of lemonade.*
	How much is that, please?
Shopkeeper (FLA)	That will be £1.50, please. How long are you staying at the campsite?
Pupil	*Another two days. Thank you very much and goodbye.*
Shopkeeper (FLA)	Have a nice holiday.

As with the first role play, the pupils need to be familiar with both roles in order to complete the role play successfully.

Activity: Noughts and crosses

Prepare a reference sheet with the text and visual cards (see opposite).

Set the pupils to work in pairs. Provide a grid of nine squares
(large enough to accommodate the visual cards).

Task

Provide five **O**s and five **X**s on acetate per pair. The pupils decide which one is **O** and which is **X** and divide the acetate squares accordingly. The pupils place the cards face down in a pile.

Partner 1 places nine cards face up on the grid. Each in turn chooses a card on the grid and has to say what the a card represents. If correct the pupil places his/her corresponding acetate O or X on top of the card.

The first one to achieve a line of Os or Xs is the winner. They continue the game until all the phrases have been practised.

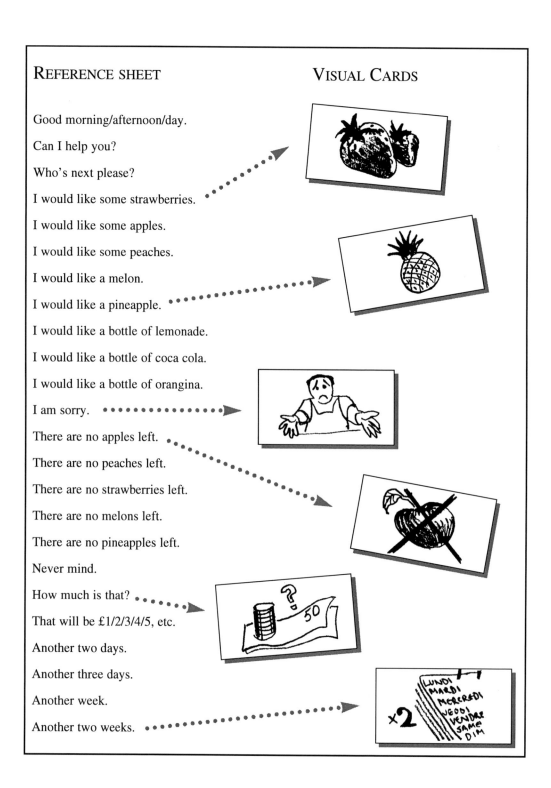

Reference Sheet

Good morning/afternoon/day.

Can I help you?

Who's next please?

I would like some strawberries.

I would like some apples.

I would like some peaches.

I would like a melon.

I would like a pineapple.

I would like a bottle of lemonade.

I would like a bottle of coca cola.

I would like a bottle of orangina.

I am sorry.

There are no apples left.

There are no peaches left.

There are no strawberries left.

There are no melons left.

There are no pineapples left.

Never mind.

How much is that?

That will be £1/2/3/4/5, etc.

Another two days.

Another three days.

Another week.

Another two weeks.

Visual Cards

Activity 2: relay race dictation

Prepare a similar dialogue to the one provided on p54 and two A4 cards. Blu-tack the two dialogues to the wall or board at opposite ends.

Divide the group into two teams of equal numbers (if unequal someone runs twice). Each team chooses a scribe who will not run but will write down what his or her team dictates (the most able writer). Say Go/Blow a whistle/Ring a bell.

The first pupil in each team has to run up to the dialogue card and memorise as much as possible. He or she returns to the team and dictates what he or she has memorised.

The next pupil in the line then runs up to the dialogue card and memorises the next part of the dialogue. The race continues until one team has finished. What the winning team has written is then checked against the OHT.

PRESENTATION AND DISCUSSION

This task requires pupils to present some aspect of their lives. This is prepared in advance.

Topics for discussion may include their family, interests and hobbies, holidays they have been on, their work experience placement.

They will provide some visual material such as a photo/some realia/souvenirs/a poster for the task. This will act as a prompt.

SPOT THE DIFFERENCE

Choose a picture/photo of a family and photocopy it enough times for pupils to work in pairs. The family can be your own or one of their pupils' or a cartoon family such as the Simpsons.

Write a text to describe the photo/picture but include deliberate mistakes.

Pupil A has the picture.

Pupil B has the text.

Pupil B has to read the text. While he or she is doing this Pupil A interrupts and says 'No, that's not right' and corrects the mistake — '**there are five people in your family**'.

Pupils now have a template which they have practised. They can now use this template to describe their own family using a picture/photo, or other groups such as the characters in *Neighbours* or *Eastenders*.

This activity can also be done using two texts without the use of a visual, where the pupils have to spot the difference.

> Hello! My name is Lisa Simpson. I would like to present my family to you. There are **seven people** in my family, myself, my mother who is called Marge, my father who is called Homer, my brother who is called Bart and my little sister who adores watching television. My brother Bart **loves playing the saxophone.**
>
> I work very hard at school, and I get very good marks. My brother does not get good marks but he **loves school all the same.** My father works in a factory and my mother works at home. My father is small and has a fat tummy unlike my mother who is tall and slim. My father **is very elegant and intelligent.** My brother **is very like him.**

PRACTICE AND CONSOLIDATION ACTIVITIES

SINGING THE 'DAILY ROUTINE' BLUES

The 'blues' offers an excellent structure for practice, repetition and creativity!

> Well I got up this morning and I was feeling so down.
> *Gap for guitar /harmonica solo or noises*
> Oh yeah, I woke up this morning and I was feeling so down.
> So I decided the answer was shopping in town, yeah shopping in town.
>
> So I took the 8 o'clock bus and I paid my fare.
> *Gap for guitar /harmonica solo or noises*
> Oh yeah baby, I took the 8 o'clock bus and I paid my fare.
> When I arrived at the shops I had no money to spare.
>
> My friends they do say 'Don't let your troubles get you down'.
> *Gap for guitar /harmonica solo or noises*
> Oh yeah ! My friends they do say 'Don't let your troubles get you down'.
> But what can you do, when you got problems all around.
>
> I know all this weeping won't help me at all.
> *Gap for guitar /harmonica solo or noises*
> Yeah don't I know all this weeping it won't help me at all.
> But every time I leave the house, another problem comes to call.

(adapted from lyrics by Duke Boy Bonner)

Task (i)

Pupils are provided with the first verse to show the structure of the blues. The other verses are cut up into strips and placed into envelopes. Each pair has a different verse (or all the verses).

In pairs the pupils put the strips into a sequence. When each pair has finished sequencing they read/sing out their verse.

Task (ii): brainstorm and write up for pupil reference

With some groups it may be necessary to start by using English, which you and/or certain pupils can then translate. They are more likely to retain language that they have contributed rather than that you provide.

- Daily routine vocabulary and structures (cf GCSE).
- Problem vocabulary and structures, i.e. *unrequited love, homelessness, the poverty trap, environmental issues, racism, sexism, violence, unemployment.*

These titles are displayed in the target language in columns on an OHP. You may not want to use all of them in one go.

The pupils work in pairs and write their own verses using their daily routine language and 'problem' language you have brainstormed as well as the lyrics provided by you.

Task (iii)

Linguistically competent pupils could be more free to experiment with the lyrics and work without the template.

Task (iv)

Encourage pupils to set their 'blues' to music!

Well I got up this morning and I _____
Gap for guitar /harmonica solo or noises
Oh yeah, I woke up this morning and I _____
So I decided _____

So I took the _____
Gap for guitar /harmonica solo or noises
Oh yeah baby, I took the _____
When I _____

My _____ they do say '_____'
Gap for guitar /harmonica solo or noises
Oh yeah ! My _____ they do say
'_____'
But what can you do _____

I know _____
Gap for guitar /harmonica solo or noises
Yeah don't I know _____
But every time I _____

THE INVITATION ROLE PLAY RAP

This is a practice or consolidation activity which can be done either with a small group or as whole class activity. In a whole class setting the class teacher can take on the role of the person inviting and the FLA that of refusing the invitation. With a smaller group you should invite one of the more confident linguists to perform the latter role.

This is another musical idiom that lends itself well to practising and performing the foreign language. Like the blues it offers opportunities for repetition, rehearsal and performance.

The pupils will have been learning the language for inviting friends out, making arrangements and accepting and refusing invitations.

Brainstorm with the pupils the expressions they know for inviting people. Then they brainstorm the places they could be invited to — you join in, translating, if necessary, what they say in English.

You write on the board/OHP for pupil reference.

Likely structures and suggestions are as follows:

The invitations

Would you like to . . .	go/going to the . . .	cinema, swimming pool, the shops,
Do you want to . . .		ice rink, café, a football match, seaside,
Do you fancy . . .		countryside, into town, horse race, round
		my house, my auntie's, for a walk,
Transport	by car/ bicycle/roller skates/ motorbike/bus.	
When?	Saturday night, tonight, tomorrow night/ afternoon/ morning, this weekend/ next weekend, at eight, six, ten o'clock, etc.	

The group then brainstorms excuses for not going. (Start off by being polite, becoming less and less polite.)

The excuses	*Polite*	*Less polite*
	I'm terribly sorry, but I can't.	I don't like . . .
	I'd love to but I'm busy, I have no money.	I'm going out with . . .
	I have to do my homework.	You must be joking.
	I have to look after my little sister/brother.	With you? Dream on.
	I have to wash my hair.	I'd rather watch the news.
	I don't feel well.	That's not possible.
	I've got the flu.	
	I have a dentist appointment.	

Using the 'brainstormed' language, you make up rhythmic phrases and practises chanting them with the pupils. The result could be something like this:

| **Inviting** | Do you fancy coming out this weekend. |
| | To the seaside with me and my friend? |

| **Refusing** | Thank you very much, you are very kind. |
| | I'm busy this weekend, I hope you don't mind. |

| **Inviting** | Would you like to come tonight, to the cinema? |
| | I'll meet you at eight, I'll bring my car |

| **Refusing** | I am sorry I've got my homework to do. |
| | I don't feel well I've got the flu. |

Divide the group into '**inviters**' and '**refusers**'. The pupils are set up to work in pairs to write two, four or six rhythmic phrases like the examples above. You circulate to help, check and provide ideas.

When the pairs have written their rhythmic phrases they read/chant them out for you to write up on the OHP, using different colour pens to denote '**inviters**' and '**refusers**'.

First the '**inviters**' feed back then '**the refusers**' and so on until all the pairs have contributed. You may need to edit the text to provide a model version. When the rap is complete the pupils are asked to chant the text after you for pronunciation purposes (use the ideas that appear on p42).

When they are confident pupils are asked to stand and chant their respective roles. You clap four times between each verse and encourage them to clap and move rhythmically! They can then practise the rap in pairs and you can circulate to monitor pronunciation and accuracy. You photocopy their 'Rap' and give a copy to each contributor.

USING GRIDS TO COLLECT INFORMATION: TALKING ABOUT THE HOLIDAYS

The group practises the following questions using text and visuals on OHP (see p42 for repetition and practice ideas):

When pupils are confident with the language, they ask each other the questions and fill in the grid. They make a note about each pupil using a grid with the following headings: Name; Where?; Who with?; How?; What they did; Weather; Did they enjoy it?

They can then use the grid like the one below to play *Who am I talking about?* Provide a model:

He went to **Spain.** He went with **his family.** He took **the plane.** While he was there, he **sunbathed, swam in the sea and swimming pool** and **played volley ball on the beach.** The weather was **hot and sunny.** He had **a great time.** *Who is it?*

This can be followed by descriptions of holiday photos or general conversation. As with the role plays, pupils need to be familiar with question and answer forms of the topic to be discussed. You provides visuals and text as with the holiday questions.

HOME AND DAILY ROUTINE

Pupils are asked to respond to the following:

- Can you describe your house? What do you do to help around the house?
- Is there any chore you particularly dislike? Do you ever prepare meals ?
- What to you normally eat in the evening? At what time do you eat?
- And with whom?

Describing your house

You provide text and visuals as a model and lead a chant as in an American soldier's marching song:

I live in a terraced house.	A kitchen where we cook and eat
Pupils repeat	*Pupils repeat*
It is on the edge of town	And three bedrooms where we sleep
Pupils repeat	*Pupils repeat*
In my house there are six rooms	There are gardens in the front and back
Pupils repeat	*Pupils repeat*
A living room and a bathroom too	I live a house, not in a flat
Pupils repeat	*Pupils repeat*

The pupils use this model to describe their own homes. They can then describe their homes without the chanting using a picture or a photo.

Talking about housework

Task (i)

You brainstorm the different types of housework and write in the chore column, then write up the other columns. Pupils fill in the grid individually. In pairs they ask each other who does what in the house.

Who does the dishes in your house?	It's usually me
Who does the cooking ?	It's usually my father
Who does the shopping?	It's usually my mother . . . and so on.

Chore	approximate time taken to complete	me	mother	father	brother	sister	other
Do the dishes							
Vacuum cleaning							
Dust and polish							
Prepare the meals							
Do the shopping							
Make the beds							
Tidy your bedroom							
Tidy the house							
Clean the bathroom							
Do the washing							
Do the ironing							

Task (ii)

Using a similar grid you collate the information to find out which pupil does the most chores at home and which pupil spends most time doing chores.

Chore	approximate time taken to complete	pupil1	pupil2	pupil3	pupil4	pupil5	pupil 6
Do the dishes							
Vacuum cleaning							
Dust and polish							
Prepare the meals							
Do the shopping							
Make the beds							
Tidy your bedroom							
Tidy the house							
Clean the bathroom							
Do the washing							
Do the ironing							

Patrick is the one who does the most chores.
Krisma is the one who spends the most time on chores.

Pupils are more likely to retain language that they can associate with people they know.

Task (iii)

The FLA prepares a grid like the one below:

Helping at home		I do already	I think I could do
In the kitchen	prepare a meal		
	do the washing up		
	tidy up and clean		
	do the ironing		
	do the laundry		
	other		
My bedroom	make my bed		
	decorate		
	clean		
	tidy		
	change the light bulb		
	other		
In the garden	mow the lawn		
	plant bulbs/seeds		
	prune		
	dig		
	other		

In this task the household chores are categorised. The pupils have to make two more choices and tick the columns as appropriate to their circumstances. They then feed back by using a template and adapting the words *in italics:*

These are the things I already do —
    In the kitchen *I do the washing up.*
    In my bedroom *I make my bed and tidy up.*
    In the garden *I do nothing.*

I think I could do more, for example
    In the kitchen I could *do the laundry and tidy up*
    In my bedroom I could *change the light bulb*
    In the garden I could *mow the lawn and maybe do some digging*

CiLT

13. GCSE activities: the written coursework

Pupils are required by some GCSE boards to complete written coursework concerning their work experience placement. Work experience is part of the curriculum in the vast majority of schools in in this country. It usually takes place in Year 10 or in some cases in Year 11.

This an experience that the overwhelming majority of pupils enjoy and do very well in. Preparation for, and feedback from, this placement can be done during language lessons to encourage pupils to talk about it in the target language.

 ## PREPARATION FOR WORK EXPERIENCE

What should I think about?		
Hours of work	At what time do I start?	
	At what time do I finish?	
	When is the lunch break?	
Travel	How do I get there?	
	How much will it cost?	
	Do I know the timetables?	
Meals	Is there a canteen?	
	Do I need to bring sandwiches?	
Dress code	Do I need to wear a tie/skirt?	
Supervision	Do I know the name of my supervisor at the workplace?	
	Do I know the name of the teacher from school?	

When work experience has taken place, a similar type of grid could be provided to practise past tenses.

Feedback template

I know what time I start and finish, but I don't know the time of the lunch break.
I shall be travelling by train, but I'm not sure yet about the cost or the timetables.
I need to find out about the dress code.
I know the name of the supervisor at the work place, but I am not sure which teacher will be supervising me.

 ## USING MATRIXES TO ENCOURAGE ASKING QUESTIONS

Prepare a matrix along the following lines, using language the pupils will have 'covered':

Matrix 1

	A. People/jobs	B. an object	C. a 'place'
1	the teacher	toothbrush	the bath
2	the pilot	toothpaste	the handbag
3	the bricklayer	towel	the suitcase
4	the waiter/waitress	meal	the garden
5	the hairdresser	cup of coffee	the wall
6	the secretary	documents	the bedroom
7	the wife	bottle of wine	the railway station
8	the husband	flowers	the airport
9	the queen	books	the castle
10	the painter	story	the bin
11	writer	photo	the blackboard
12	child	teddy bear	the overhead projector

Prepare a second **open** matrix with a framework for a question:

Why did A   put B   in/on/under/next to C ?

First of all you give out the open matrix. Ask your pupils to circle at random a number in each column. Then you give out **matrix 1.**

Using the numbers they have circled they make up questions using the framework you have provided, e.g.

Why did A put B in/on/under/next to C?

The pupils in turn put their bizarre questions to you (or to each other if they are able).

A	B	C
1	1	(1)
2	2	2
3	3	3
4	4	4
5	5	5
(6)	6	6
7	7	7
8	8	8
9	9	9
10	10	10
11	(11)	11
12	12	12

Matrix 2

Example: Why did the secretary put the photo in the bath?

You provide an answer! . . . *because it was dirty!*

The pupils record the replies — they can then use the matrix again and ask different, 'surreal' questions. Abler pupils may even be willing to take on your role.

14. Other Key Stage 4 activities

 I OFFER MY GIFT TO . . . (ENCOURAGING PROCRASTINATION)

You distribute small scraps of paper and tells the pupils to write down a 'gift' consisting of five words that they would like to give to another member of the group, e.g. a bouquet of red roses, a red and black Ferrari, a box of Belgian chocolates, a beautiful silver mountain bike. When all have written down their gifts you collect them and redistributes them. The pupils read their new gifts and in turn choose a member of the group to whom they will offer this gift. They must explain why that person would want such a gift. The explanation should last as little as 30 seconds or as much as one or two minutes according to the pupils' linguistic competence.

This activity is ideal for encouraging pupils to use 'redundant' language. Below are some examples in English. You should make a list of these types of expressions in your own language.

- *delayers*   'Well, let me see', 'right then', 'OK' and 'er um'

- *contact establishers*   'You know (what I mean)', 'as I was saying', 'where was I?' 'In fact'

- *affective starts*   'Has she really started school already? How time flies.'

- *remark in parenthesis* 'What did I do with my pen?' 'Where is the worksheet?'

The following is an example of pupils' explanations:

Well, let me see, *I offer X a beautiful silver mountain bike because she loves riding bicycles and likes to go for rides in the country side, in town and at the seaside. She likes sport,* you know, in fact *she loves sport, especially cycling and she wants to keep fit.* As I was saying *she's very sporty and she loves the colour silver. With this beautiful silver mountain bike she will be able to visit her friends and use it to come to school, so it will save her money, etc.*

 ALIBI I

A crime has been committed last Saturday evening between 7 and 11pm. You decide with the group what type of crime it was. Two pupils are sent out of the room, they will be the detectives and must work out questions to ask the suspects. You and the rest of the pupils decide who has committed the crime. All of pupils are the suspects. Those pupils who are innocent have sound alibis. The 'criminal' has an alibi that is contradictory. The detectives are invited back into the room and have to find out who is the 'criminal'

Questions such as 'Where were you? What were you doing? Who with?', etc should be prepared on paper in advance. It may be helpful for you to play the role of one of the detectives initially in order to demonstrate some model questions at an appropriate level.

ALIBI II

In this case two pupils are chosen to leave the room to prepare an alibi which will render them beyond suspicion for a crime which took place the previous evening. They have five minutes to agree a version, including a considerable amount of detail, e.g. 'We went to an Indian restaurant, we arrived at eight o'clock there were two waiters. Becky had a chicken tikka and I had prawn Madras, we both drank Coke, etc. We left the restaurant at 10.15 and she caught a bus while I walked home . . .

While the two students are preparing their alibi you prepare with the rest of the class a number of questions designed to test their alibi, e.g. 'What were you wearing? What was she wearing? What was the weather like? Was the waiter friendly? What number was the bus?', etc.

The two suspects are called back into the room one by one and interrogated individually for, say, three minutes by the rest of the group, each of whom has at least one pre-prepared question to ask. At the end of both interrogations the group decides whether there is sufficient conflict of evidence to prosecute — and there usually is!

You should select competent and confident pupils as the first suspects in this activity and will need to be aware that the rest of the group may need considerable help in devising appropriate questions. This is intended to be very much a 'fun' activity and, as recommended previously, the stress should be on communication rather than strict grammatical accuracy, but you may wish to make a note of any recurring errors for subsequent reference.

15.   A guide to developing creative language

 ### DEVELOPING THE LEARNERS' CREATIVE 'RUCKSACK'

For pupils to use language creatively they require confidence as well as some linguistic competence. From the outset they need to be encouraged to 'play around' with language, and build their personal 'creative rucksack'. Within every class, whatever the level of linguistic competence, there is enormous potential for using the pupils' imagination to develop creativity. However, we need to provide them with structures as starting points. These structures will give them the confidence to enable them to 'play around' with language. Creative writing is an excellent support to oral confidence and competence.

When planning creative outcomes always ensure an oral focus. If they write a poem, they recite it, if they write a 'rap' they rap it, if they write a song they sing it, if they write a story, they tell it.

Creative writing can follow a pattern:

A motivation to write
What is the purpose? Who is the audience? Is the content of their writing meaningful to them?

A stimulus for the imagination
This can be a photo, a painting, a song, a joke, a poem, a video clip from a film, an advert. In fact the stimulus can be almost anything. Be provocative!

Brainstorming of vocabulary and structures
A useful way of doing this is in categories. This will be mainly 'pre-learned' language. However, you can contribute as well since this will extend their vocabulary. At this stage it is sometimes appropriate to accept some English usage, you can then provide the foreign language equivalent.

Form
Initially you provide the form, but as the pupils' 'creative rucksack' begins to fill, they can begin to choose the form.

Dictionaries
It is a requirement of the National Curriculum that all pupils use dictionaries, and they can be extremely useful. For guidance on their use in the MFL classroom see Pathfinder 28: *Making effective use of the dictionary*.

Presentation method
How will they present their work? Will it be to the small group, or to the whole class? Will it be 'published' in a booklet? Will they use the OHP? Will they need to learn it by heart?

First draft

Pupils do this in pairs. A blank page can be very daunting. Working collaboratively in this way will give them greater confidence to fill the 'blank page'. They can either go on to produce a collective creative effort as with the Rap described on p59, or they can produce a joint effort in pairs.

Reviewing, revising and editing

Encourage the pupils to check their work for accuracy and meaning. Encourage them to read out loud to see if it sounds 'good' or right. They will need help and guidance, as they may not have developed sufficient linguistic awareness to do this. Stick to the target language when giving advice.

Rehearsal

It is important that opportunities are provided for the pupils to rehearse. Encourage them to use props, music, movement and dance to enhance their performance. They will need to work on pronunciation and intonation in particular.

Presentation and publication

The pupils present their work to their audience, their group, their class or in an assembly. Their work can also be compiled in a class book which can be read by other groups of pupils.

Audience response

By presenting and publishing their writing, the work they do in foreign languages is given a higher profile. This will boost their confidence and help them to develop positive attitudes to the foreign languages that they are learning.

 ## IDEAS THAT HAVE WORKED IN THE CLASSROOM

SETTING LANGUAGE TO WELL-KNOWN TUNES

The pupils simply change the words *in italics*

Tune: 'We shall not be moved'
I don't have
I don't have *a dog*
I don't have
I don't have *a dog*
I have *a cat*
I have *a rabbit*
But unfortunately
I don't have *a dog*

ACROSTICS

You or the pupils choose a word or phrase such as *'My friend'*. The pupils write down the word or phrase vertically and use the brainstorm and dictionaries to compose their own poem:

M aria is my best friend
Y ellow is her favourite colour

F riendly and funny
R eally funny
I like her a lot
E xceptional
N ever lets you
D own

CINQUAINS

Poems made up of five lines constrained by a syllabic structure.

Line 1	two syllables	Listen
Line 2	four syllables	Like the flutter
Line 3	six syllables	Of a butterfly's wings
Line 4	eight syllables	The perfumed velvet petals fall
Line 5	two syllables	Around

OCTOPOEMS

Describe a person or an object using this eight-line formula. The line 'titles' will be determined by the topics covered by the pupils. The pupils can choose a famous person, a pop or film star, their best friend a member of their family or a pet.

This poem works equally well without the italics. The simpler form could be used by the less confident linguists. You could also choose a four-, five-, six- or seven-line formula.

Nelson Mandela

1	Colour	Nelson Mandela is green, *hope for the future*
2.	Season	He is Spring *a new beginning*
3.	Place	South Africa *new and young*
4	Clothing	A cotton shirt *multicoloured*
5.	Weather	Sunny *bright and warm*
6.	A drink	A fruit juice *cool and refreshing*
7.	A type of food	An orange *full of zest*
8	A type of music	Jazz and soul *calypso*

DAILY ROUTINE BLUES

In this poetry version, the pupils change the phrases in italics, using the language brainstormed earlier.

Like I usually do

I get up a seven
like I usually do
Then *I have a wash*
like I usually do
I get dressed in my bedroom
like I usually do
I drink my coffee

like I usually do
I leave the house
like I usually do
I take the tube at eight o'clock
like I usually do
I arrive at school
like I usually do
But you are not there
So I do not smile
like I usually do

IF ... WAS A ... , ... WOULD BE A ...

Choose your **'topics'** according to the language your pupils have covered. In this case it is toys, colours, animals, musical instruments and numbers. You then brainstorm the vocabulary as outlined in the guidelines.

If my sister were a **toy**
She would be a *ball*
round and bouncy
If she were a **colour**
She would be *red*
like an apple
If she were a **pet**
She would be a *kitten*
cute and full of life

If she were a **pop star**
She would be *Michael Jackson*
because she is 'bad'
If she were a **musical instrument**
She would be *a drum*
VERY noisy
If she were a **number**
She would be a *1*
'Happy Birthday Madeleine'

MATHEMATICAL POEMS

More syllabic verse:

My brother
2 Patrick
4 He loves cycling
6 Kind and very funny
8 likes playing music very loud
6 because he is fifteen
4 fair haired blue eyed
2 brother

YOU SAY YOU ... BUT ...

You say you love *animals*
But you eat them
You say you love *flowers*
But you pick them
You say you care about *the environment*
But you drop litter
So when you say that you love me
I am not sure.

Pupils change the words in italics.

TO WRITE A LOVE STORY

Follow the same pattern as in the guidelines below, but divide the group into pairs or threes (up to ten), each of which deals with one or two parts of the story.

The parts

1 The meeting (Who? Where?)
Decide on the characters — physical description

2 Love strikes (Both at the same time? At different times?)
More description including qualities/ jobs/ where they come from/ hobbies

3 Love grows (Both in love now)
Dialogue — I love you, I will never leave you, etc

4 Love overcomes the difficulties * in its path (Events? Location?)
Exams, homework, moving house, from different cultures

5   Love overcomes its enemies **   (People — hostile relatives/jealous rivals)
    Parents/friends against the match because age , exams, class ,culture

6   Love wins. All seems well, but . . .
    Spend some time together, a festival, a school trip

7   Love is hurt by the difficulties (same as * above or different)
    More or the same problems arise again

8   Love is hurt by its enemies (same as ** above or different)
    People interfere

9   Love is lost
    One loses his/her love

10 Love separates with/without bitterness
    They go their separate ways

A CIRCLE SONG

Brainstorm jobs/professions/people vocabulary and write up descriptions. Make sure you include the jobs/people that appear in the story — teacher, doctor, mother, musician.

Alternatively you can prepare descriptions of different jobs/people, e.g. 'Someone who serves the dishes in a restaurant or a café' (waiter/waitress), 'Someone who looks after sick people (nurse). The pupils then give you the names of the jobs.

The pupils work in pairs and use the poem to write their own version by changing the words in italics:

Once upon a time there was a story	It was told to a *mother*
It was not a long story	*Who gave it a big hug*
It was a short story	It was told to a *musician*
A good story	*Who played it on her flute*
It had neither beginning nor end	It was told to me
First of all the story was told to a child	And I took it
The child said 'tell me it again'	And I placed on a tree
The story was told to a *teacher*	And that's the story
Who wrote up on the blackboard	Once upon at time there was a story
The story was told to a *doctor*	It was not a long story
Who examined it carefully	It was a short story
The story was told to an *artist*	A good story
Who painted it into her canvas	It had neither beginning nor end

Appendix 1: Code of conduct for assistants — an example

- Be punctual at all times.

- In case of illness, sickness or other absence notify the department before 8:30.

- Prepare lessons in advance as requested.

- Try to speak in the target language with pupils at all times.

- If working with small groups,try to stay on task at all times.

- Refer any discipline problems to the head of department.

- Be prompt for meetings with individual teachers and your mentor.

- Do not hesitate to ask for help or advice.

- Let your mentor know of any problems or difficulties you are having.

- Try to become fully involved in school life.

- Enjoy your year.

FLAs will be expected to work within the philosophy of the department and are expected to carry out the following duties:

- plan and prepare for their appointed sessions;

- keep appropriate registers and records;

- liaise effectively with all teachers they support;

- teach in accordance with the schools equal opportunities policy;

- play a full role in the cultural life of the school, including extra curricular activities.

Appendix 2: Session plan guide — an example

FLA session plan guide

Class	Date	Length of session

Linguistic Objectives :   (**R**evision/Consolidation)

    pupil to pupil | instructions | Topic

Outcomes: **Resources:**

by the end of the session the pupils will be able to

Timing	Activities
Notes on session	

Appendix 3: References and further reading

Barkat M and Y Lefranc, *La boîte à outils de l'assistant de français* (London: Service Culturel, French Embassy, London, 1997)

Barkat M and Y Lefranc and B Hill, *La boîte à outils* (video) (London: CILT and French Embassy, 1997)

Berwick G and P Horsfall, *Making effective use of the dictionary*, Pathfinder 28 (London: CILT, 1996)

Byram M and G Zarate, *Young people facing difference* (Strasbourg: Council of Europe, 1995)

Channel 4 Schools, *Working together*, training video and notes: Programme 1: the FLA in the classroom; Programme 2: strategies for group work (Warwick: Educational TV Company, PO Box 100, Warwick, CV34 6TZ, 1993)

Halliwell S and B Jones, *On target*, Pathfinder 5 (London: CILT, 1991)

Jones B, *Exploring otherness*, Pathfinder 24 (London: CILT, 1995)

Langran J and S Purcell, *Language games and activities*, Network 5 (London: CILT, 1994)

Leeds LEA: *Working with your foreign language assistant — a handbook for schools* (Leeds LEA 1997, draft) available through Leeds LEA Advisory and Inspection Publishing Dept, 0113 214 4068

Horsfall P, *Advanced vocabulary French/German/Spanish* (Cheltenham: Mary Glasgow Publications, 1994)

McColl H and S Thomas, *Cartoons for classroom communication* (London: Miniflashcards, 1997)

Page R, *Working with your foreign language assistant* (Cheltenham: Mary Glasgow Publications, 1997)

Seegar H, *Praktische Unterrichtstips für Assisstenten im vereinigten Königreich* (London: Goethe Institut, 1993)

Snow D and M Byram, *Crossing frontiers*, Pathfinder 30 (London: CILT, 1997)

Spanish Embassy, *Actividades para la clase de español elaborados por auxiliares de conversación*

Wright A, *1,000 pictures for teachers to copy* (London, Collins 1984)

Appendix 4: Useful addresses

AMBASSADE DE FRANCE, SERVICE CULTUREL

Bureau de Coopération Linguistique et Educative, 23 Cromwell Road, London SW7 2EL.
Tel: 0171 838 2055. Fax: 0171 838 2088

CENTRAL BUREAU FOR EDUCATIONAL VISITS AND EXCHANGES (CBEVE)

London office: 10 Spring Gardens, London SW1A 2BN. Tel: 0171 389 4004.
Fax: 0171 389 4426

Edinburgh office: 3 Bruntsfield Crescent, Edinburgh EH10 4HD. Tel: 0131 447 8024
Fax: 0131 452 8569

Belfast office: 1 Chlorine Gardens, Belfast BT9 5DJ. Tel: 01232 664 418. Fax: 01232 661 275

The Central Bureau makes available a number of circulars concerning FLAs, including 'Notes for FLAs' (SD/N100) and 'Notes for schools and colleges receiving FLAs' (SD/N101).

CILT (CENTRE FOR INFORMATION ON LANGUAGE TEACHING AND RESEARCH)

Resources Library, 20 Bedfordbury, London WC2N 4LB. Tel: 0171 379 5110.
Fax: 0171 379 5082.

*Information sheets available for quick reference use; free on receipt of a large (A4) stamped addressed envelope. In particular No 7: Directory of language associations and organisations for schools, No 27: European awareness: organisations, projects, resources;
No 36: Europe and language teaching: policy issues*

GOETHE-INSTITUT

London: 50 Princes gate, Exhibition Road, London SW7 2PH. Tel: 0171 411 3431.
Fax: 0171 581 0974

Manchester: 4th Floor, Churchgate House, 56 Oxford Street, Manchester, M1 6EU.
Tel: 0161 237 1077. Fax: 0161 237 1079

York: County House, 32-34 Monkgate, York, YO3 7RQ. Tel: 01904 611 122.
Fax: 01904 612 736

SPANISH EMBASSY, EDUCATION OFFICE/CONSEJERIA DE EDUCACIÓN

20 Peel Street, London W8 7PD. Tel: 1071 727 2462. Fax: 0171 229 4965

ciLT